The Catholic Ideal: Exercise and Sports

The Catholic Ideal: Exercise and Sports

Robert Feeney

AQUINAS
PRESS

Cover photo by Arturo Mari, L'Osservatore Romano

Photo credits:
Papal pictures - Photo Service, L'Osservatore Romano.
Pictures of Pier Giorgio Frassati - Wanda Gawronski, Rome, Italy.

*Dedicated to Mary, the sweet and caring Mother of God,
who in simplicity and love watches over and smiles on
her children
at play and at prayer,
and to John Paul II, God's athlete and Mary's Pope.*

Acknowledgements

Special gratitude to Mary, the sweet, caring, and loving Mother of God, for all that she has been and continues to be in my life. To her who has been spiritually at my side with her help and inspiration in the enjoyment and fun in the writing of this book. To her, I give the fruit, the good that will come from it. Special appreciation goes to Cardinal George Pell for his Foreword. Thanks go to those who gave their endorsements: Cardinal Paul Poupard, Archbishop Timothy Dolan, and Archbishop Elden Curtiss. Special thanks go to the Office of Church and Sport at the Vatican for assisting in obtaining papal pictures. Thanks go to Wanda Gawronski, the niece of Blessed Pier Giorgio Frassati, for the pictures of her uncle.

Contents

Prefatory Note

I found *The Catholic Ideal: Exercise and Sports* absorbingly interesting. It is a handy compendium of Catholic doctrine culled from the teaching of the Popes and offers excellent practical tips on the benefits of regular daily exercise. I like the holistic approach of dealing with the human being as wonderfully made up of body, mind, and spirit, endowed as it is with dignity since the Word became flesh and assumed a human body.

At a time when international matches are reportedly fixed, dope tests are carried out on athletes, body parlors are crowded, and some types of sport are so highly commercialized as to risk even the health and lives of the contestants, this work strikes the right balance by putting the whole field of exercise and sports in a truly Catholic perspective. I warmly recommend this book to all those engaged and interested in physical education and pray that it will significantly influence the culture of sports and physical fitness.

+ Paul Cardinal Poupard
President, Pontifical Council for Culture
Vatican City

Foreword

Although many people still suffer in our world, it is undoubtedly true that many enjoy a greater level of comfort and security than their ancestors. Yet how many of us waste our leisure by turning personal comfort into a life of indolence or inactivity? Where life is easy, it is tempting to become lazy, slothful, to lose aspirations, fail to expand horizons or make connections with other people - in short, it is tempting to stop being active.

Robert Feeney's book reminds us of the Catholic tradition of the body, the integrated human person, on looking after our health, cooperating with each other, and competing in sport and games, not just in war or trade.

Sport and exercise are parts of life in which we can strive for goals and for victory in peace and with respect for each other. This is obviously preferable to victory through violence or through dishonesty and unfairness. Where sport is clean, open, friendly, and from a position of rough equality, individuals, and especially youngsters, benefit enormously. And those of us whose sporting activities have slowed down somewhat can gain too by spectating the attempts of participants to excel, to support teammates and honour rivals, and to accept defeat or victory with grace and dignity.

I commend Robert Feeney's attempt to explain the distinctively Catholic view of sport. Where others denigrate the body, the Church upholds the body's dignity but refuses to reduce the human person to body alone. Where others promote winning at any cost, the Church teaches the great virtues such as temperance, courage, justice, hope, faith, and speaks up for human character that is based on these qualties. Where individualism reigns, the Church proposes communal effort and social responsibilities, while always safeguarding the individual's rights. Where play and sport are reduced to winnings or contaminated by drugs, the Church reminds us that the prize in the only race that ultimately matters is eternal life, and that cheats compromise their honour and their chances of ultimate happiness.

Recently, Pope John Paul II established a department of *Church and Sport* intended to explore and inspire fairness, integrity, and legality in sports. As Robert Feeney shows, this development arises from a strong interest of the modern Church in physical exercise and sport. This collection of Catholic wisdom on the active life of the body is timely indeed and will surely prove helpful to Catholic coaches and sportspersons, and to everyone interested in healthy play and honest competition.

+ George Cardinal Pell
Archbishop of Sydney

1

Exercise and Sports in the Service of the Soul

I n this book the reader will come to understand why the Holy
Catholic Church so highly values physical exercise and sport,
as well as the contributions they make to the integral development of the human person. Research in exercise physiology and
sports medicine provides substantial evidence that all of us need
to be physically active in order to prevent hypokinetic disease,
which is associated with a sedentary way of life. This book will
introduce to the reader the benefits of exercise and sports, while
helping you to set up not only a personal exercise program, but
one for your family.

In this book the reader will be introduced to the teachings
of the Doctor of the Church, St. Thomas Aquinas, along with two
great popes, Pius XII and John Paul II. These teachings will help
us to reconstruct our view of exercise and sports and to understand
them as a means of perfecting the body – an instrument of the
mind – in the search for and communication of truth. This book
will also show how exercise is a means of relieving tension and
stress, as well as a useful way to be more patient, loving, and open
to the pursuit of truth.

The reader will also be introduced to the importance of
being "spiritually fit," recalling St. Paul's reflections on sports

and exercise in his epistles, which emphasize the struggle for our imperishable reward – that is, the eternal life with God. In 1993, John Paul II talked about how St. Paul compared two types of athletes – athletes of sports and athletes of the Faith. This book offers the reader a wholesome prescription for spiritual fitness, as well as for physical fitness. The athlete of sport uses exercise and nutrition to build strength for physical competition. The athlete of the Faith uses prayer and the sacraments to build up spiritual strength to meet the challenges of life.

There is a great need for the sports world to be evangelized, and this requires theological reflection on the Christian message as it applies to sporting activity. Like the runners of old, the reader of this book can pass the torch to others, so that the champions of sport today and in the future will participate with an enlightened Catholic concept of exercise and sports.

The nature of man bids us not to disconnect spiritual functions from bodily functions. An early Father of the Church, St. Irenaeus, states:

> For that flesh which has been moulded is not a perfect man in itself, but the body of a man, and a part of a man. Neither is the soul itself considered apart by itself, the man, but is the soul of a man. Neither is the spirit of a man, for it is called the spirit, and not a man; but the commingling and union of all these constitutes the perfect man.[1]

Before the advent of Christianity, the Greek philosophers Socrates, Plato, and Aristotle advocated for physical fitness as a means of bringing body and soul into harmony with each other. Those Greek philosophers and their civil leaders placed a great value on physical activity and mental cultivation. The gymnasium was a place where men exercised the body and heard lectures of orators and philosophers. Plato declared:

> . . . that God, I should say, has given man
> the two arts, music and sports. Only incidentally
> do they serve soul and body. Their purpose is to
> tune these two elements into harmony with one
> another by slackening or lightening, till the proper
> pitch be revealed.[2]

In *The Republic*, Plato argues that physical exercise is the twin sister of the arts for the improvement of the soul.

In the fifth century B.C., the Greeks spent one hour daily in the gymnasium. Socrates is reported to have said:

> No citizen has a right to be an amateur in
> the matter of physical training; it is a part of his
> profession as a citizen to keep himself in good
> condition, ready to serve his state at a moment's
> notice. Finally, what a disgrace it is for a man
> to grow old without ever seeing the beauty and
> strength of which his body is capable. And in all
> the uses of the body, it is a great importance to
> be in as high a state of physical efficiency as
> possible. Why even in the process of thinking, in
> which the use of the body seems to be reduced to
> a minimum, it is a matter of common knowledge
> that grave mistakes may often be traced to bad
> health. (*Memorabilia* 111-12)

Aristotle had the notion that "To a good bodily constitution corresponds the nobility of the soul" (*II De Anima*, lect. 19).

In 776 B.C. the Olympic Games were started in Olympia, which is in the southern peninsula of Greece, 210 miles southwest of Athens. These games were strictly amateur, and the final prize was a beautiful wreath. The tradition was to hold the games every four years in honor of the pagan god Zeus. The visitors in the stadium, located at the foot of Mt. Kronion, gave public thanks

*The 211-meter track in Olympia (above) is where
the 200-meter foot race was run in the first
Olympic Games in 776 B.C.
The starting block is pictured below.*

The athletes walked underneath this stone arch in Olympia (above), which dates back to 776 B.C., on their way to the track.

to Zeus, the king of the pagan gods, as well as other deities. In Olympia there was a temple to Zeus which was home to a forty-foot statue of Zeus, considered one of the "seven wonders" of the ancient world.

The only event associated with the Olympics in 776 B.C. was the 200-meter foot race, run on a straight 211-meter track. It was won by a cook named Coroibos. In 724 B.C. the 400-meter run was added to the initial race, and in 684 B.C. a long distance race of 4,600 meters was included. In 708 B.C., wrestling and the pentathlon were added. The pentathlon demanded many skills of an athlete because it included five events – discus throwing, jumping, javelin throwing, running, and wrestling. Their training developed in the pentathletes supple bodies admired by many, including Aristotle (384-322 B.C.), who said:

> Each age has its own beauty. In youth, it lies in the possession of a body capable of enduring all kinds of contests. It is for this reason that pentathletes are the most beautiful; they are naturally adapted both for exertion of the body and swiftness of foot.[3]

New events were added until 520 B.C., at which time the Olympic program was complete. This program endured for many years thereafter.

The Roman Emperor Constantine the Great accepted Christianity around 313 A.D. and made it the faith of the Roman Empire. In 391 A.D., all pre-Christian cults were banned by Emperor Theodosius of Rome. The Olympic Games were discontinued in 394 A.D. by Emperor Theodosius because the athletes had begun to demand money, and corruption had become a problem.

Sports as they were played by the Greeks in gymnasiums did not appeal to the Romans. The Romans were more spectators than participants, preferring spectacles such as gladiatorial contests held in the Roman Coliseum, built in 82 A.D. with a capacity of 50,000. The Christians eventually came to condemn these contests for the unnecessary bloodshed they entailed, and the contests were abolished by official decree in 404. The Romans also enjoyed chariot racing, and these were held in hippodromes such as the Circus Maximus in Rome, which could hold 200,000 spectators.

Roman citizens engaged in exercise more for health than for competition. The Campus Martius served as a playground for Roman citizens – a place where they could run, jump, and playfully wrestle. If physical activities such as swimming, running, and wrestling were not militarily practiced, Roman boys tended not to engage in them. Roman soldiers were trained in running, jumping, swimming, spear throwing, archery, and wrestling.

By the 1100s, peasants played various kinds of handball and ball games using a stick. Historical records indicate that every ball game known to modern man has its roots in medieval times. The Church encouraged the playing of games as forms of rest and re-creation of strength. Tennis had its beginnings in medieval times, starting as a kind of handball played by monks, abbots, priests, and bishops. In the fifteenth century rackets were first strung with strips of sheep intestine, representing the beginning of racket sports. Knights engaged in exercise for self-protection and self-preservation during warfare. The feudal aristocracy devised tournaments consisting of jousting, which kept knights ready for battle.

During the Renaissance (1400-1600 A.D.), the Humanists embraced physical education and sports with the enthusiasm of the classical Greeks. They were attracted to the Greek ideal of the harmony and unity of body and soul. Many people played sports and excelled in the arts during this period, which was considered

St. Ignatius Loyola encouraged physical activities for physical fitness. He promoted the use of these activities to build strong and healthy bodies, to glorify God, and to reach greater spiritual and moral goals.

the era of the scholar-athlete. Games and exercise that developed muscles and posture were encouraged, and the idea of the whole man, "the Renaissance," incorporated physical as well as mental development. During the Renaissance tennis was regarded as the "sport of kings." St. Thomas More, Erasmus, and Shakespeare all refer to tennis in their writings.

Aeneas Sylvius Piccolomini, a Humanist who would become Pope Pius II (1458-67), wrote treatises declaring the complimentary relation of a sound mind and a healthy body. He constantly encouraged physical exercise and sports during his papacy. He viewed the habits developed through physical exercise and sports as beneficial for body and soul throughout the lifespan. St. Ignatius Loyola too encouraged physical activities for physical fitness. He promoted the use of these activities to build strong and healthy bodies, to glorify God, and to reach greater spiritual and moral goals.

Johann Friedrich Guts Muths (1759-1839) of Germany is regarded as one of the founders of modern physical education. He wrote and published the first manual on physical education. Not since the Greeks had anyone treated the subject of physical education more intelligently. Homer, in his epics *The Iliad* and *The Odyssey*, gives us the earliest knowledge about the physical sporting activity of the Greeks. Competitive sport in modern times is a sort of refinement of the physical contests of these ancient and medieval traditions.

The Catholic Church is interested in exercise and sports because the human body is, as St. Paul states, the temple of the Holy Spirit. The Church views the body as having its part to play, like the soul, in giving homage to God. The Church prizes everything that serves the harmonious development of the body, the masterpiece of all creation. In this way, a sense of respect for the competitor and for fair play is developed, as well as for the spirit and body being trained for effort, sacrifice, brotherhood, and courtesy. The Church wishes to help us form an attitude of exercise and sports as practices not simply for their own sake – they are not to be raised as idols. The Church wishes to see sport transformed into an instrument for the elevation of man toward the supernatural goal to which he is called by God.

So often today we encounter people who emphasize the care of the body at the expense of moral and spiritual development. As the former Archbishop of Philadelphia, Cardinal Anthony Bevilacqua, has stated,

> In our Western culture, especially, we are surrounded daily by a fascination and often an obsessive pursuit of self-esteem through physical accomplishments. Many young men and women use sport competitions, body building programs, weight control regimes, as well as cosmetic or plastic surgery as means to heighten their worth in today's world. In all his writings and in so many of his public addresses, our Holy Father has consistently emphasized the dignity of the human person as created in the image and likeness of God. In addresses that the Holy Father has given to athletes on numerous occasions, he has given us a vision of sports based on the principle that the dignity of the human person is the goal and criterion of all sporting activity.[4]

St. Paul viewed our bodies as temples of the Holy Spirit. He encourages us in his epistles to cultivate the dignity and harmony of this temple. Much of St. Paul's life reflects a strength and vitality that enabled him to endure the trials of his missionary travels. In his journeys to Corinth, Greece, he witnessed the Isthmian Games, which were held regularly there at the Isthmus of Corinth, connecting northern and southern Greece. The enthusiasm for athletic spectacles there seems to have made a deep impression on him. The sanctuary of Poseidon, where the games

The excavated sanctuary of Poseidon in Corinth, Greece is where St. Paul witnessed the Isthmian Games.

were held, has now been excavated. St. Paul refers to sports activity in order to point out the spirit of courage demanded by the Christian life – a life much like that of a demanding sport, directing a person's energies toward the perfection of character. He invites us to "fight the good fight of faith" (1 Tim 6:12) and not to be discouraged by obstacles.

St. Paul's personality derived much from his Greek background, with its emphasis on athletics. His hometown of Tarsus had a stadium where games were held, as well as a gymnasium on the banks of the River Cydmus. St. Paul appears to have had a great interest in sports. He visualized the Christian life as an athletic contest, and the vocabulary of athletics appears in his epistles as a powerful metaphor. For example, in 1 Cor 9:24 he writes: "Do you not know that in a race all the runners compete, but only one receives the prize. So run that you may attain it." The Church values this New Testament passage as giving athletes not only motivation to win the contest, but also to win the contest of knowing the meaning of life and the purpose of our human existence, along with realizing that union with God is the ultimate victory, the eternal crown.

In the document *Gaudium et Spes*, the Second Vatican Council (1962-65) spoke of physical exercise and sports as ways of fostering friendly relations between peoples of all classes, countries, and races. The Olympic Games are one example of how sports can provide opportunities for encounters between people of different nations and cultures. For example, Pope Paul VI spoke of the Olympic Games as a way of learning to confront each other in the peaceful struggles of the stadium and on the court, rather than in the battlefield.

After being discontinued in 394 A.D., the Olympic Games were revived in Athens, Greece on April 6, 1896. With 50,000 spectators looking on, King George I of Greece formally opened the first of the modern Olympic Games. The Panathinaiko stadium was the main venue for the major events of this first modern Olympics. There were 245 athletes from 13 countries participating in 42 events in 10 sports. The first Olympic marathon race was held at that Olympics, and 16 men ran in it. The marathon was inspired by the legend of the messenger Phidippides, who was said to have run 24.8 miles from Marathon to Athens in 490 B.C. to announce, in his dying breath, a Greek victory over the Persians in the Battle of Marathon. A 24-year-old Greek shepherd and farmer, Spiridon Louis, won the first marathon race in two hours and 58 minutes. The standard distance of 26.2 miles for the marathon began in the 1908 London games.

The man most responsible for the modern Olympic Games being revived in 1896 was Baron Pierre de Coubertin (1863-1937), who had complete support of Pope St. Pius X. Coubertin, a French Catholic, was convinced that the Olympic Games could improve international peace, brotherhood, and understanding. His dream was of the youth of the world coming together in peaceful and wholesome competition. Coubertin invited many interested individuals to a Sports Congress held at the Sorbonne at the University of Paris in 1894. The event closed with a resolution to revive the Olympic Games.

Coubertin made a study of the value and impact of sports on society, and his investigation included 12 trips to England between 1883 and 1887, as he studied the British sporting philosophy. He was greatly influenced by the British educationalist Thomas Arnold, who was headmaster of the Rugby School from 1828 to 1842. He was also inspired and influenced by the French Dominican priest Henri Didon, O.P., who suggested to Coubertin the idea that would become the Olympic motto: "Citius, Fortius, and Altis," or "Faster, Stronger, and Higher." Didon was headmaster of a French high school named St. Albert the Great, located in

This monument in Marathon, Greece shows where the messenger Phidippides started his 24.8-mile run from Marathon to Athens in 490 B.C. It inspired the marathon race.

Arcueil, near Paris. The motto Coubertin would use was written on the entrance to Fr. Didon's high school. The Catholic Archbishop of Athens, Nicolaos Foskolos, in his homily at the Mass opening the 2004 Olympic Games in Athens, mentioned the Dominican priest Didon and his motto, along with John Paul II's opening of an Office of Sports in the Vatican just before the Athens Olympics began.

Coubertin founded and wrote a monthly newspaper, the *Athletic Review*, in an effort to increase interest in sports. In 1889 he traveled in the United States and Canada, visiting high schools and colleges such as Stanford, Princeton, Tulane, and the University of California to observe the games and sports played there. Too, it was Pierre de Coubertin who designed the Olympic flag that has flown above the Olympic Games since 1920. The five colored rings intertwined on the flag symbolize the five continents from which the athletes came every four years to compete. Pierre de Coubertin died in 1937. He was so fond of Olympia, the village where Greek athletes competed from 776 B.C. to 393 A.D., that he asked that his heart be sent there after his death. Coubertin admired the greatness of the ancient Greeks and their high esteem for athletic vigor. He admired their delight in the human body, as well as in the human mind. Today his heart rests beneath a marble column monument atop a hill overlooking Olympia. His body is buried in Lausanne, Switzerland, home of the International Olympic Committee – an organization for which he served as the first president.

The 26th Olympic Centenary Games were held in Atlanta, Georgia 100 years after the games were revived in Athens in 1896. They were held between July 19 and August 4, 1996. In his message to the athletes of those games, Cardinal Pio Laghi, then Prefect of the Congregation for Catholic Education , referred to Pope Blessed John XXIII:

Pier de Coubertin's heart rests under this marble column monument, atop a hill overlooking Olympia.

I remember those beautiful words of John XXIII when he addressed the athletes of the Rome Olympic Games on August 24, 1960. The Pope sought then to remind them that it was impossible to separate their striving for the full expression of their bodily resources from an increasingly profound perception of the spiritual values connected with sporting activity. He said that there was an undoubted need to take care 'that in sporting competitions, all aims be not centered on the body alone as man's supreme asset; and let not passion for sport obstruct the complete fulfillment of our duties.' But he did not fail to stress at the same time the benefits, bodily and spiritually together, to be derived from athletic commitment. In fact, the Holy Father said: 'There can be no doubt either that we must always appreciate and encourage the honest physical exercises and noble competitions of the gymnasium. And numerous and of great value are the gifts and advantages that develop in man through sporting competitions; as regards the body: health, vigor, agility of limb and grace; but as regards the soul: constancy, strength, the exercise of personal sacrifice.' [5]

Athens, Greece celebrated the world's return to the birthplace of the modern Olympic Games on August 13, 2004. The theme of the games was "Welcome Home," and the Olympic flame arrived at the Parthenon on August 11 after having traveled 50,000 miles around the world with 33 stops in 26 countries. On August 13, some 10,000 athletes from 202 countries were introduced to the 72,000 spectators who gathered at the Panothinaika, where the first modern Olympics had been held in 1896.

The shot-put event took place on August 18 in Olympia, and it was the first time an athletic event had taken place in Olympia since 393 A.D. There were no bleachers in ancient Olympia as the 15,000 spectators sat on the grassy slopes overlooking the stadium, which now contains ruins including stones

Athens, Greece celebrated the world's return in 2004 to the birthplace of the modern Olympic Games. The theme of the games was "Welcome Home."

The Panothinaika stadium (above) in Athens is where the first modern Olympics was held in 1896. The 2004 Olympic venue is pictured below.

that mark the first starting line from 776 B.C. The original stadium measured 211 meters by 32 meters and had a crowd capacity of 40,000. Athletes walked underneath a stone arch dating to 776 B.C. The medalists wore wreaths from an olive tree growing amid the ruins. It has been written that Olympia, today a village of 1,200 residents, is a place that settles the soul. It is surrounded by beautiful cypress, pine, and laurel trees.

The Olympic Games there concluded on August 29, 2004. Earlier that month, on August 8, Pope John Paul II had stated:

> In a few days the 28th celebration of the Olympic Games will be inaugurated in Athens. I send my cordial greetings to the official delegations, to the national representatives, to the athletes, and to all who will be taking part in the Olympics. As I remember the cordiality with which the Greek people welcomed me on the occasion of my pilgrimage in the footsteps of the Apostle Paul, I would also like to greet with special warmth the City of Athens. I deeply hope that in the world today, disturbed and sometimes overwhelmed by so many forms of hatred and violence, the important sports events of the games will be an opportunity for a friendly encounter and will serve to further peace and understanding among the people. Upon the Olympics and upon the whole of the world of sports I invoke the maternal protection of the Most Holy Virgin.[6]

Just prior to the Athens 2004 Olympic Games, Pope John Paul II, who was dubbed "God's athlete" early in his papacy, instituted a new section within the Pontifical Council for the Laity, entitled "Church and Sport," in order to ensure on the part of the Holy See a more direct and organic attention to the vast world of sport. A few days after the establishment of this new office was publicly announced, John Paul II on August 8 entrusted the 2004 Athens Olympic Games and the whole world of sports to the loving protection of Mary, the Mother of God. The Vatican noted that the Olympic Games in Athens, with its millions of spectators from around the world, was but another manifestation of the prominent place that sport occupies in the lives of so many people in our society. The Church, which has always been concerned with all spheres of human activity, is also called to concern itself with the world of sport.

The office of Church and Sport serves as a point of reference for and dialogue with various national and international sports associations and organizations in order to promote an authentic culture of sport, in harmony with the dignity of the human person. Attentive especially to those particular challenges of an ethical nature that involve especially professional sports, this new section will seek to shed light on these concerns, as well as promote other initiatives that assist in proclaiming the Gospel to the world of sport, especially through the fostering of authentic Christian witnesses among professional athletes.

The Vatican press release stated that the world of sport is at a crucial moment in its history. As various sports disciplines today have a tendency to stray further and further from their original ideals, the Vatican said it was all the more urgent to reclaim for sport its fundamental values and purpose. In light of this, the office of Church and Sport has been entrusted with the following aims:

1) To be a point of reference in the Church for the various national and international sports organizations;

2) To help the local Church to be attentive to the importance of her pastoral care in this field, and at the same time favor collaboration among various Catholic sports associations;

3) To promote a culture of sport as a means of the integral development of the person and at the service of peace and fraternity among peoples;

4) To conduct studies about specific themes concerning sport, especially from an ethical perspective; and

5) To organize and promote initiatives that foster the witness of an authentic Christian life among sports professionals.

The new office would like to draw attention to the numerous speeches and writings that various Pontiffs have offered to sports men and women who have come to Rome to encounter the Pope, especially (but certainly not exclusively) in the pontificate of Pope John Paul II, who presided at a Jubilee of Sport at Rome's Olympic stadium in the Holy Year of 1984, as well as during the Great Jubilee of 2000. These discourses, while on the one hand soberly warning about the extremes that should be avoided in the practice of sport, on the other hand highlight the educational and formative function that sport, when practiced correctly, can play in the cultivation of human virtues, as well as providing a sort of ascesis for the spiritual life. The Vatican's new department hopes to be an impetus for others to rediscovering such fundamental values as hard work, dedication, fairness, sacrifice, loyalty, and teamwork.

To contact the Vatican's office of Church and Sport, write to: Office of Church and Sport, Pontifical Council for the Laity, 00120 Vatican City, Europe – or send email to sport@laity.va.

2

A Sound Mind in a Sound Body

A sound mind in a sound body is an ideal that can make an individual worthy of the description once applied to St. Thomas Aquinas: "an orderly exposition of what a man should be, delightful to God and man."

St. Thomas Aquinas, Doctor of the Church, was born in 1225 in the family's castle high upon the hill of Roccasecca, Italy. Physically, Thomas was extremely strong and feared nothing. He was robust and tall, most likely 6 ft. 3 in. His eventual travels and the long walks he undertook are estimated to have covered some 9,000 miles on foot, which argues for him being robust. His face was tanned, with refined and handsome features. The mother of Thomas's companion and secretary Reginald reported:

> When Thomas was passing through the countryside, the people who were working in the fields left their labors and ran to meet him, admiring the imposing stature of his body and the beauty of his human features. They went before him more indeed because of his beauty than on account of his sanctity or noble origin.[7]

Thomas was the Dominican teacher par excellence. He received his master of theology (doctorate) degree in 1256 from the University of Paris and also taught there for a number of

The remains of the family castle where St. Thomas Aquinas was born in 1225, high upon the hill in Roccasecca, Italy, midway between Rome and Naples.

years, where he was a popular instructor. An early biographer writes that "When Thomas entered upon his duties as teacher and began disputations and lecturing, students flocked to his class-room in such numbers that the hall could hardly accommodate all of them."[8] Thomas didn't just want his students to be knowl-edgeable – He wanted them to be the teachers of others. His writings were many, and he is principally known for his masterpiece theological work, *The Summa Theologica*. More than any other theological text, it enjoys the approbation of the teaching authority of the Church. Next to the Bible and official Church teachings, there is no book that is comparable in its theological importance.

Thomas died at age 49 on March 7, 1274 at the Cistercian Abbey of Fossanova. Pope John XXII canonized him on July 18, 1323, saying: "Thomas alone has illuminated the Church more than all the doctors together." Pope Benedict XV wrote that "the Church has proclaimed that the doctrine of St. Thomas Aquinas is her own." In 1880, Pope Leo XIII made Thomas's philosophy and theology the basis of Catholic education. He encouraged Catholic teachers to make the explanation of Christian doctrine by St. Thomas the basis for all of their instruction.

In honor of the seventh century after the death of St. Thomas in 1974, Pope Paul VI honored him by going to the Abbey of Fossonova in Italy, where Thomas had died. He also visited Roccasecca, Thomas's birthplace. Paul VI wrote a letter, "Lumen Ecclesiae," for the seventh centenary. In it, he states that "In philosophical and theological studies, he is a guide whom none can replace. Go to Thomas; seek out and read the works of St. Thomas."[9] Pope John Paul II had praised Thomas as a model for the modern philosopher and theologian, as St. Thomas stressed the dignity of man in his writing and teaching. John Paul II gave St. Thomas the title "Doctor of Humanity."

Thomas drew heavily on Aristotle's world view and philosophy. He subscribed to Aristotle's notion that "to a good bodily constitution corresponds the nobility of the soul." Aquinas considered taking care of the body a virtue and a sign of wisdom. Exercise and sports as means of relieving tension and bringing rest to the soul were part of St. Thomas's philosophy. In Aquinas's commentary on Aristotle's Nicomachean Ethics, he comments on man's need to rest from bodily labors and to relax the mind from serious pursuits by means of play. Today, experts in exercise physiology back up this philosophy and tell us that our muscles need to relax, as it is part of their function. Doctors in the field of sports medicine recommend physical activity and sports for tension release. Many of them believe that exercise and sports serve better than pills as a tranquilizer for the release of tension, thus enabling the muscles to relax. In our everyday life we are affected by many irritants, both interior and exterior, ranging from personal problems to traffic jams, from the ringing of telephones to the noise of the radio or television. Studies have shown that after exercise, electrical activity in the muscles is lower, making them more flexible and relaxed.

Ronald M. Lawrence, M.D. and Ph.D., noted in the field of sports medicine and physical fitness, asserts that as you do aerobic exercise your brain produces endorphins, hormones that help relieve nervous tension. William Menninger, M.D., a noted psychiatrist and founder of the Menninger Clinic in Topeka, Kansas, encouraged physical activity as an outlet for instinctive aggressive drives by enabling the individual to "blow off steam," leading to relaxation and supplementing daily work. Additionally, Cardinal Edmund C. Szoka, a runner and president of the Vatican City State Commission, has stated that "Any kind of exercise is good for you. It helps you to relax, get rid of anxieties, worries, disappointment, or anger."[10]

St. Thomas Aquinas viewed physical exercise as medicine

*St. Thomas Aquinas viewed exercise as medicine for the
soul and a suitable means to refresh a tired mind.
He considered taking care of the body a virtue
and a sign of wisdom.*

for the soul and as a suitable means to refresh a tired mind. In book three of the Summa Contra Gentiles, St. Thomas states that sports and exercise have a proper end – namely, that after our minds have been relaxed by the activity, we may be better able to do serious jobs. As contemporary studies have shown, aerobic exercise can improve a person's intellectual capacity. Reports have shown that with exercise comes greater originality of through and duration of concentration. Exercise increases the blood supply to the brain, and with this increase the brain receives more oxygen. The result is that individuals find they may think more clearly after exercise. John Paul II remarked that we can develop through long hours of exercise and effort the power of concentration and the habit of discipline. Ray Killinger, M.D., indicates in his report on aerobic exercise that:

> Aerobic fitness results in improvement in the following categories of the thinking process: originality of thought, duration of concentration, mental response time, ability to change topics and subjects quickly, depth of thinking, duality of thought – the ability to entertain a number of ideas at once, and finally, mental tenacity.[11]

Sports and exercise can perfect the body as an instrument of the mind and can help the mind in its search for and communication of truth. The Greek philosophers had beliefs about the body and soul that should not surprise us. We know that thought comes as a result of long preparation, during which the entire body is at work. Our experience is the result of the senses and the operation of the intellect that depends upon the senses. The eminent late Dominican Fr. A.G. Sertillanges, O.P., wrote that:

> Minds can only communicate through the body. Similarly, the mind of each one of us can only communicate with truth and with itself

through the body. So much so that the change by
which we pass from ignorance to knowledge must
be attributed, according to St. Thomas, directly to
the body and only accidentally to the intellectual
part of us.[12]

Kenneth Cooper, M.D. of the Aerobics Center in Dallas,
Texas, is convinced that being physically fit can help produce
psychological fitness. John Paul II saw sports and exercise as
means for the body to reach optimum physical condition, which he
believed brings marked consequences for psychological wellbeing.
This is particularly important. After all, St. Thomas Aquinas taught
that contemplation is man's highest activity. And Joseph Pieper, a
German disciple of St. Thomas, wrote a book titled *Leisure, the
Basis of Culture*. In this text Pieper describes contemplation as
man's greatest happiness. Aerobic activity, which has been shown
to increase oxygen into the body, can definitely aid us in contemplation.

St. Thomas Aquinas's position and teaching on exercise
and sports helps us to see the potential intellectual gains that can
come from exercise and sports. His teaching on psychosomatic
unity helps us to have a deeper appreciation for the value of
physical fitness and the development of physical skills, as well
as for the perfecting of sensory experience to help us acquire
knowledge. St. Thomas speaks to our times, since we desperately
need a reconstructed view of sports and exercise as a way to
perfecting the body as an instrument of the mind – ultimately
important for helping the mind in its search for and communication of truth.

St. Thomas also speaks to our times because of the great
increase of different forms of automation and the need for physical
exercise to relieve tension and restore a healthy balance to mind
and body. John Paul II witnessed to the great need people have for

exercise in the contemporary world, stating:

> In an age that has witnessed the ever increasing development of various forms of automation, especially in the workplace, reducing the use of physical activity, many people feel the need to find appropriate forms of physical exercise that will help to restore a healthy balance of mind and body.

Pope Pius XI's idea of exercise and sports was to rest the mind and prepare it for new work, much like St. Thomas Aquinas. The idea that Pius XI had of exercise and sports was expressed by Pope Pius XII thus:

> To exhaust the body within healthy limits in order to rest the mind and prepare it for new work, to sharpen the senses in order to acquire greater intensity and penetration in the intellectual faculties, to exercise the muscles and become accustomed to effort in order to temper the character and form a will as hard and elastic as steel.[13]

Pius XI, dubbed the "Alpine Pope," was described by Pius XII as a "master of mountaineering." Pius XII would speak of Pius XI's 20-hour climb of Mt. Rosa in northern Italy and of how this Pope demonstrated a great tenacity that helped him carry out the many demands of his papacy. Pius XI was the first Italian to make the difficult ascent of Mt. Rosa to the summit of the Dufour Peak. He conquered the most dangerous peak of the Alps. During his papacy, people commented on his great physical energy and physical conditioning. Pius XI described his experience as a mountaineer as one of irresistible attraction to heights and the healthy attraction to difficulties to be overcome. He writes that "True mountaineering is love for nature and her most hidden treasures. It calls for prudence, courage, strength, and fortitude."[14]

Pius XII strongly believed that the ancient adage "a sound mind in a sound body" should become widely realized, but he also encouraged great compassion for those who are not able to enjoy wellbeing through exercise and sports. He wanted everyone to know that human dignity and human duty are not limited by this adage, and that there is nothing to prevent a soul, even a great and heroic one, from being housed in a weak or impaired body. Pius XII taught that those who are physically compromised and unable to take part in exercise and sports are fulfilling a mysterious design of God Almighty – and that their nobility of soul is to be shown by not only avoiding envy of those who can participate in sports, but also in sharing in their joy. Pius XII encouraged healthy and robust people to be of service to their sick brethren: "Bear one another's burdens, and so you will fulfill the law of Christ" (Gal 6:2).

Pius XII taught that exercise and sports are an effective antidote to softness and easy living, and that they lead man to moral strength and greatness. The Church values sports and exercise as virtuous when practiced in proper proportion. St. Thomas Aquinas wrote of the virtue of fortitude as that which makes reason prevail over exhaustion and physical pain. One of the true values of sports and exercise is in helping one to overcome obstacles, an aspect of the virtue of fortitude. On the occasion of the Jubilee for Sport on October 29, 2000, John Paul II stated in remarks at Rome's Olympic Stadium: "This altar, placed in Rome's great Olympic Stadium, has reminded us that sports too are above all God's gift. This gift now asks to become mission and witness."[15]

Philosopher Paul Weiss, who once taught at the Catholic University of America and authored *Sport: Philosophic Inquiry*, saw man's concern with excellence and his effort to perfect himself as the basic features of sport. Weiss understood sport as the testimony of what man can accomplish through disciplined control of his body. The Greeks called these arête, referring to achieving a personal best. In 1896 the modern Olympic Games were reinstated with the Olympic Creed. It stressed that the most important thing in the Olympics is not to win but to take part, not to have conquered but to have fought well.

Aristotle and Plato stated what has come to be known as the cathartic theory of physical activity: "Preoccupation and expenditure of energy in physical activities help to extirpate vice and direct toward constructive rather than immoral ends."[16] Pope Paul VI seemed to echo this theory when he spoke of how athletic commitment provided an effective antidote to the idleness and laxity that usually constitute fertile ground for all sorts of vice.

It is our responsibility to do all we can to keep healthy, since the body affects the mind so directly. The early third century Father of the Church, Clement of Alexandria, states in his treatise *The Instructor* that his two main concerns include keeping healthy and becoming holy. He was a Christian apologist, a Greek theologian, and a mystic. He was the head of the Catechetical School of Alexandria in Egypt. Clement advocated physical education and sports as worthy pursuits, valuing exercise for its health benefits and its ability to aid in the wholesome development of character. He taught that individuals should carefully select exercises for individual needs. The great English churchman Cardinal John Newman saw the importance of including physical education in a liberal education. In his book *The Idea of a University*, Newman suggests that bodily exercises be undertaken because they form and cultivate the intellect – not because of utilitarian reasons.

The Catholic Church has confronted false teachings about the body throughout her long history. The Manichaean heresy of St. Augustine's time condemned the body, believing it to be bad. On October 22, 1980, John Paul II stated that "If the

Manichaean mentality places an anti-value on the body and sexuality, Christianity teaches that the body and sexuality 'always constitute a value not sufficiently appreciated.' In other words, if Manichaeism says the body is bad, Christianity says 'the body is so good that you can't even fathom it.'"[17] We are called to care for and love our bodies and to respect them as temples of the Holy Spirit. St. Paul teaches us about the need to show this respect to the body in 1 Cor 6:19: "Do you not know that your body is a temple of the Holy Spirit within you which you have from God? You are not your own; you were bought with a price. So glorify God in your body." *The Catechism of the Catholic Church* states that "The flesh is the hinge of salvation. We believe in God who is creator of the flesh; we believe in the Word made flesh in order to redeem the flesh; we believe in the resurrection of the flesh, the fulfillment of both the creation and the redemption of the flesh" (1015). The *Catechism* teaches us to perceive our own bodies and the bodies of others as "a temple of the Holy Spirit, a masterpiece of divine beauty" (2519). Too, it teaches us that the Catholic Church has had to defend the dignity of the body and the goodness of the physical world throughout her 2,000-year history.

In the teachings of John Paul II, especially the "theology of the body" talks he gave between 1979 and 1984, he continually reminded us that the body expresses the individual person as a loving person, imaging the Trinity. The *Catechism* states it so well: "God has revealed his innermost secret: God himself is an eternal exchange of love, Father, Son, and Holy Spirit, and he has destined us to share in that exchange" (221). John Paul II taught us that the body is the means by which we freely make a gift of ourselves to God and to another, a self-donation for the good of the other. God created our bodies male and female so as to image his love in marriage, making ourselves a sincere gift to each other and becoming "one flesh." John Paul II taught us that our body is a vehicle made for union and communion, and in this we must realize our likeness to God. Likewise, the Second Vatican Council taught that man can only find himself through a "sincere gift of self."

The world of physical education and sports greatly needs this vision of the body offered by John Paul II. This vision can influence the way we view exercise and athletics and the way we treat each other, train for sports, and play our games. John Paul II implemented the thoughts of St. Thomas Aquinas and the German philosopher Max Scheler in broadening our vision of the body as God's masterpiece, capable of making visible what is invisible: the spiritual and the divine. John Paul II used aspects of phenomenology, a modern philosophical method founded by Edmund Husserl (1859-1938), in broadening our vision of the body. Phenomenology is not some abstract notion of what a given phenomenon is "in itself," but is precisely the given phenomenon as it is experienced or "as it appears" – the description of the experience, its qualities, characteristics, and structures. Karol Wojtyla immersed himself in the study of phenomenology to begin his research on ethics in 1951. John Paul II was among the most outstanding representatives of our time in the field of phenomenology. His thesis for his second degree was concerned with erecting a Christian ethic on the principles of Max Scheler, who applied phenomenology to the world of values, establishing an objective hierarchy with material values at the bottom and religious values at the top.

The thirteenth century was a time when the Albigensian heresy taught that the body was evil. The Albigensians believed that all life on earth, being the work of Satan, was inherently bad. The Albigensians renounced the sanctity of marriage and the procreation of children, and suicide was considered praiseworthy because it put an end to the body. This anti-life attitude produced a culture of death marked by no respect for the dignity of human life. At the core of this heresy, which St. Dominic described as the "child of the devil," there lay what John Paul II called "a denial of the Incarnation, a refusal to accept that the 'Word was made flesh and dwelt among us, full of grace and truth'" (Jn 1:14).

St. Dominic (1170-1221), author of the Rosary, Mary's athlete, and founder of the Dominican Order in 1216, confronted the Albigensian heresy by stressing the truth of the Incarnation and the body. Dominic taught the Rosary – a Christocentric, Marian, and contemplative prayer – as a means of teaching Gospel truths (especially the Incarnation and the dignity of the body). The Rosary was Dominic's weapon, his antidote to the false beliefs concerning the body. The Rosary has been continually promoted by the Church, and especially by the Dominicans, since Dominic's time. The prayer was promoted and emphasized by John Paul II throughout his papacy, especially during the *Year of the Rosary*, October 2002-2003. He wrote an apostolic letter on the Rosary (see appendix) during that year. In this letter he says:

> The Rosary is a prayer loved by countless Saints and encouraged by the Magisterium. It is destined to bring forth a harvest of holiness. With the Rosary, the Christian people sits at the School of Mary and is led to contemplate the beauty of the face of Christ and to experience the depths of his love.

Jansenists, Puritans, and Victorians of recent centuries have also had an influence on the development of an unhealthy attitude toward the body, reviving in part the attitude of the Albigensians. St. Augustine writes that "Man is to be taught, too, in what measure to love his body, so as to care for it wisely and within due limits, but no one is to be told not to desire the safety and health of his body because there is something he desires more."[18] This St. Dominic and St. Thomas Aquinas understood; this contemporary Albigensians must not forget.

Blessed Pier Giorgio Frassati, a handsome, healthy, and robust Italian athlete who strived for physical and spiritual fitness. John Paul II in 1984 called him "model of athletes."

3
Pier Giorgio Frassati: Model Athlete

Pope John Paul II encouraged athletes to acknowledge their physical talents and sporting achievements as a gift of God himself and to give glory to God the Creator through their athletic accomplishments (1 Cor 6:20). John Paul II encouraged athletes to realize that being in the public eye, they are responsible for setting high standards of sportsmanship and personal excellence, especially to the young, who look to athletes as role models.

John Paul II gave an inspiring sermon on October 29, 2000 in Rome's Olympic Stadium, on the occasion of the Jubilee for the World of Sports. At the end of the sermon, he prayed:

> Lord Jesus Christ, help these athletes to be
> your friends and witnesses to your love. Help them
> to put the same effort into personal asceticism
> that they do into sports; help them to achieve a
> harmonious and cohesive unity of body and soul.
> May they be sound models to imitate for all who
> admire them. Help them always to be athletes of
> the spirit, to win your inestimable prize; an imper-
> ishable crown that lasts forever. Amen.[19]

The words contained above in the prayer recited by John Paul II fit perfectly Blessed Pier Giorgio Frassati (1901-1925), a handsome, healthy, and robust Italian athlete who strived for physical and spiritual fitness. John Paul II saw Blessed Pier Giorgio, whom he beatified in 1990, as a model to inspire the athletes of our day. John Paul II made mention of him in 1984 on the occasion of the International Jubilee for Athletes in Rome's Olympic Stadium. He stated:

> You have models to inspire you. I am think-
> ing, for example, of Pier Giorgio Frassati, who was
> a modern young man open to the values of sport.
> He was a skillful mountaineer and able skier, but
> at the same time he bore a courageous witness of
> generosity in Christian faith and charity towards
> others, especially the very poor and the suffer-
> ing.[20]

In Pallone, Italy in 1989, John Paul II said of Pier Giorgio:

> For my generation he was a great inspira-
> tion. Even I, in my youth, felt the positive influ-
> ence of his example. As a student, the force of
> his Christian witness made a great impression on
> me.[21]

It is said of the young people who worked on the staff of World Youth Day in Toronto, Canada in 2000 that they would often say of Pier Giorgio:

> This cool, handsome athlete is someone like
> us . . . he knows our struggles. He suffered with
> his family situation and he struggled with personal
> relationships. He loved his friends. He was nor-
> mal.[22]

Blessed Pier Giorgio Frassati was born on April 6, 1901 in Turin, Italy. He was the only son of Alfredo and Adelaide Frassati. His one sister was named Luciana. When he was a young boy, his mother would take her children on beautiful mountain walks in the Alps near Turin. His father, who was the founder and director of the liberal newspaper *La Stampa*, loved to play all kinds of

Pier Giorgio was a very lively and active child. His dear mother, Adelaide, took him and his sister on beautiful mountain walks in the Alps near Turin. He is seen here with his snow shoes on.

games with Pier Giorgio and his sister. He was a very lively and active child who was attracted to noisy toys, soccer, and bicycling. He gave himself the nickname "Dodo." As a child, he loved praying the Rosary. He would pray every night at the foot of the bed with a Rosary in his hands, until he fell asleep. As a boy, his father introduced him to horseback riding, and later he became quite a horseman. He also spent many summers at the beach by the Mediterranean Sea, where he learned to swim. He would later become a great swimmer. As a young boy, he always seemed to be in a good mood. His family called him "the life of the party." He had a very compassionate nature that went out to the sufferings of others.

Pier Giorgio was educated in public schools and also attended the Social Institute school run by the Jesuits. After school he would go to soccer practice, where he found an outlet for his pent up feelings and energy. He had a great passion for soccer and was a great player. He played forward and had dreams of joining the national team, Juve of Turin. It was at the Jesuit school that he developed the wonderful habit of attending daily Mass and receiving the Eucharist. For him, Communion was the energy to face the day, the strength to master his passions, every difficulty, and the way to overcome every obstacle to right living. In later years, he said in a speech to the Catholic Youth of Pollone:

> Feed on this Bread of Angels and from it you will gain the strength to fight your inner battle, the battle against passion and all adversaries, because Jesus Christ has promised to those who feed on the Holy Eucharist eternal life and the graces necessary to obtain it.[23]

He would often go into a church and sit in adoration before the Blessed Sacrament and speak to his best friend and the *Teacher*

Pier Giorgio and his sister, Luciana, did many things together. They were very close and enjoyed each other's company. Here you see them skating. Pier Giorgio is age 10.

*As a boy, Pier Giorgio's father, Alfredo,
introduced him to horseback riding,
and later he became quite a horseman.
Here you see Pier Giorgio on his father's horse.*

who spoke to his heart.

Pier Giorgio was never the scholarly type in school, as he never really felt comfortable in the classroom. His sister Luciana stated in her book that during his school years, the Rosary was his consolation and his weapon. Pier Giorgio would often ask friends to pray the Rosary with him. His father was an agnostic, and when he saw his son praying he considered it wasted time. When it came to the faith, Pier Giorgio was self-educated because of the family situation at home.

In his teenage years, he had a real zest for living and was very outgoing. He had a happy temperment and was very friendly. Along with sports, he was keenly interested in drama, art, music, and photography. He also really enjoyed playing pool and was a rowing enthusiast. He had a great love for skiing down the Alps near Turin with his friends. Pier Giorgio seemed fearless, and his friends admired his speed down the mountain and would often say, "He flies like the wind."

His love for Mary, the Mother of God, was strong and natural. He consecrated his whole being to her, his body and soul. He was truly Mary's athlete. His strong love for her was revealed in his tremendous love and devotion to the Rosary, and also in his early morning runs to the Marian Consolata Shrine in Turin. When he was seventeen, Pier Giorgio joined the Confraternity of the Rosary, which was originated by St. Dominic, the author of the Rosary, in the thirteenth century. At the beginning of summer, the family would leave Turin for their house in the mountains of Pallone. He would frequently hike up to the mountain sanctuary of Our Lady of Oropa to attend Mass and pray the Rosary. As he descended from the mountain shrine, he would pray the Rosary aloud and sing the litany of Mary. Today in the shrine there is a picture of him as a handsome young man wearing a suit and holding and praying the Rosary. John Paul II visited this shrine on

From his mountain home in Pallone, Pier Giorgio would hike up to the mountain shrine of Our Lady of Oropa (above). There he would attend Mass and pray the Rosary. On the way down the mountain, he would pray the Rosary aloud and sing the Litany of Loreto.

*Pier Giorgio had a great love for skiing down the
Alps with his friends. His friends would say
of him, "He flies like the wind."
Pier Giorgio (center) is seen here at age 23.*

July 16, 1989 and said:

> To those who are devoted to Mary, espe-
> cially young people like Pier Giorgio Frassati, who
> used to come up here to give himself to prayer,
> the Blessed Virgin proposes to be a shelter and a
> refuge, the heavenly Mother who opens her house
> to give everyone the invigorating experience of a
> more profound contact with God.[24]

Pier Giorgio graduated from high school in 1918 and then enrolled in the mechanical engineering program at the Royal Polytechnic University in Turin. He also joined the St. Vincent de Paul Society. He greatly loved and cared for the poor, the under-privileged, and the sick. "He loved the poor with Christ's eyes," his sister Luciana wrote in her book, *A Man of the Beatitudes.* He tried to impress upon the young that the foundation of our religion is charity, and that our lives should be shaped by the two commandments: to love God with all our strength, and to love our neighbor as ourselves. He visited hospitals and helped veterans coming home from World War I, as he truly helped so many poor and oppressed people in Turin.

The bicycle was his delight. He greatly enjoyed his 50-mile bike rides with his friend Carlo Bellingeri. He was also an ardent mountain hiker and was greatly attracted to mountain heights. In his lifetime, Pier Giorgio went on 44 mountain hikes. John Paul II has stated: "For every one of his mountain hikes, Pier Giorgio had drawn up an itinerary to accompany his ascetic and spiritual trip, a school of prayer and adoration."[25] He belonged to the Italian Alpine Club and the "Mountain Youth," an organization of young Catholics who worked at stressing the spiritual aspect of mountain hiking. His climbing of high mountains showed his personal strength, physical toughness, and stamina. The majesty of God was nowhere more apparent to him than on the heights of

Pier Giorgio really enjoyed riding a bicycle. It
was a delight. He greatly enjoyed his 50-mile bike
rides with his friend Carlo Bellingeri.
Here you see him with a bike at age 14.

mountains, especially Mt. Blanc. Some say John Paul II was like Moses, who prayed on the mountain for the Church and people of the world. John Paul II has also been referred to as theologian of the mountain. On his visit to Mt. Blanc on September 8, 1986, he said:

> Before the majestic sight of these mighty peaks and this immaculate snow, one's thoughts rise spontaneously to Him who is the Creator of these wonders: 'Always and forever you are, O God.' Throughout history, humanity has considered the mountains as a privileged experience of God and of his incommensurate greatness. Man's existence is precarious and changing, that of the mountains stable and enduring: an eloquent image of the immutable eternity of God. On the mountains, the chaotic noise of the city is silenced and quiet dominates the limitless space: a quiet in which man can hear more clearly the interior echo of the voice of God. Looking at the mountain peaks, it seems as though the earth desires to touch the sky; mirroring man's own longing for transcendence and the infinite.[26]

Pier Giorgio felt close to God in the mountains. They were a refuge for him and he saw God's smile reflected in them. He once said to his friend Marco, "How can you not believe in God when you look at all this?"[27] John Paul II had stated: "The mountains bear witness to the greatness, the strength, and the beauty of God."[28] On August 21, 1994, John Paul II visited Cogne, Italy, a little town where Pier Giorgio daringly explored the mountain peaks towering over it. There the Pope said:

> Pier Giorgio confided to his friends, 'Every day that passes, I fall more desperately in love with the mountains. I am more determined to climb the mountains, to scale the mighty peaks, to feel that pure joy which can only be felt in the mountains.'

Pier Giorgio was an ardent mountain hiker. His climbing of high mountains showed his personal strength, physical toughness, and stamina. Mountains were a refuge for him. He saw God's smile reflected in them. Here you see him descending a cliff at age 24.

The Pope ended by saying: "May this virtual contemporary of ours, Pier Giorgio, be an example to all those who go to the mountains."[29] Pope John Paul II had also said: "The mountains are a challenge; they provoke man, the human person, the young and not only the young, to make an effort to surpass himself."[30]

In 1924, Pier Giorgio and some friends founded the "Shady Characters Society" as a way of bringing together young Catholics who shared a love for hiking in the mountains. The "shady characters" prayed for each other and helped each other in their anxieties and problems. Pier Giorgio was always organizing trips to the mountains for his friends. He loved taking pictures of the beautiful scenery and also collected rocks to take back with him. His sister once said that Pier Giorgio liked the mountains because they were an answer to the dangers of city life. He also thought that trips to the mountains would keep the young from being bored and having nothing to do - and therefore out of trouble. He believed that mountain hikes teach people discipline and help develop an iron will that does not bend, so as not to fail in God's projects. Pier Giorgio was convinced that sports in general, and mountain hiking in particular, build character and discipline. His brother-in-law, Jan Gawronski, stated: "Pier Giorgio had through sports taught himself to endure physical pain, fatigue, and other discomforts as a way to be ready for whatever comes."[31] To the delegates of the Italian Alpine Club on April 26, 1986, John Paul II said:

> It is true that sporting activity, by developing and perfecting the physical and psychological potential of man, contributes to a more complete maturing of the personality, it is particularly so for those who practice alpine climbing and live it with respect for the ideals which it inspires and feeds.[32]

Pier Giorgio's Catholic faith was strong, as he nourished it through prayer. The true secret of his spiritual life was prayer. People who knew him never forgot the impression that Pier Giorgio in prayer made on them. His grandmother's nurse once saw Pier Giorgio's face glow with light as he prayed alongside his bed. He was truly molded by the Holy Spirit, who was the key to Pier Giorgio's having such a balanced and well rounded personality. In 1920, he became a night adorer, one who would spend several hours praying in church during the night, adoring the Risen Christ present in the Blessed Sacrament. His sister wrote in her book that "the Eucharistic Christ was his sovereign Lord, whom he never ceased to adore."

He loved reading spiritual books and encouraged others to do the same. His favorite reading material included the Gospels, the Epistles of St. Paul, the Confessions of St. Augustine, the life of St. Dominic, the life and writings of St. Catherine of Siena, Dante's *The Divine Comedy*, and in the year he died he began studying the works of St. Thomas Aquinas.

In May of 1918, Pier Giorgio entrusted his entire life to Mary, the Mother of God, and prayed that she would watch over him and defend him as if he were her own precious property. He would be her "devoted athlete." A friend, Marco Beltromo, once stated: "The surest means by which Pier Giorgio achieved his union with the Lord, the secret of his spiritual life, was his total devotion to Mary."[33] Pier Giorgio always had a Rosary in his pocket. He said one day while taking his Rosary out, "I carry my testament in my pocket." Pier Giorgio prayed the Rosary every day. He would pray it walking along city streets and in streetcars. He would often be found on the train praying the Rosary in front of people, and they were amazed to see such a handsome, strong, and athletic young man praying the Rosary. He would invite those around him to pray the Rosary, and because of his serene and convincing manner, they did not refuse him. Once a person saw him with a Rosary in his hand and said: "Pier Giorgio, you have become a fanatic!" He responded, "No, I have remained a Christian." When he would go hiking in the mountains with his young friends, he would always say, "Let us pray the Rosary." When there was no priest able to offer Mass at the mountain hostel, Pier Giorgio would always suggest praying the Rosary. When he and his friends from the Catholic movement *Catholic Action* would stand up for Catholic social teaching and be attacked for it, he would hold up his Rosary and call on everyone to pray for themselves and those who were attacking them. The Rosary was truly Pier Giorgio's weapon.

In 1918, Pier Giorgio was introduced to Dominican spirituality. He was very fond of reading the life of St. Dominic,who founded the Dominican Order in 1215. St. Dominic is called the "author of the Rosary" by the papal tradition of the Church. It was to Dominic that Mary first gave instruction on the Rosary and, as Pope Benedict XIII said, "St. Dominic received a command from the Queen of Heaven to preach the Rosary to the people." Pier Giorgio was convinced that God was calling him to the life of a lay Dominican. At the age of 21, he took the white scapular of the Third Order of St. Dominic on May 28, 1922 at St. Dominic's Church in Turin.

He was a true disciple of St. Dominic in encouraging the praying of the Rosary, as all Dominicans are called by the Church to be the Dominic of their times in praying and promoting the Rosary. Pope Leo XIII entrusted the Dominican Order with the express mission of promoting the Rosary. He stated: "This devotion is the rightful property of the Dominican family and to the Friar Preachers is entrusted the commission to teach it to the Catholic world."[34] Pope Benedict XV in his encyclical on June 29, 1921, stated: "We wish all Dominicans to make it their

On May 28, 1922, at the age of 21, Pier Giorgio took the white scapular of the Third Order of St. Dominic. In 1923, he professed final vows as a lay Dominican in the Chapel of Our Lady of Grace (above) in the Church of St. Dominic in Turin. He was deeply touched, as tears could be seen coming down his face. He greatly treasured being a lay Dominican.

particular task to familiarize Christ's flock with the use of the holy Rosary."[35] Pope Pius XI was fond of saying that the Rosary is the principle and foundation on which rests making perfect the life of all Dominicans and obtaining the salvation of others.

Pier Giorgio greatly treasured being a lay Dominican (tertiary) as he energetically worked at cultivating the spirit of the Dominican Order. He really worked at living the Dominican motto: "to contemplate and pass on the fruits of your contemplation to others." He enjoyed reading the life of St. Catherine of Siena, also a lay Dominican. He gave his sister a book on St. Catherine of Siena's life at her graduation, with the wish that it might guide her in her ascent toward spiritual perfection.

In 1923, Pier Giorgio professed final vows as a lay Dominican. This was done in the Chapel of Our Lady of Grace in St. Dominic's Church in Turin. He was deeply touched, as tears could be seen coming down his face. In 1922, Fr. Martino Gillet, O.P., Master General of the Dominican Order, visited Turin and remembered the impression a number of the university students who were lay members of the Order made on him. He remembered especially Pier Giorgio and later stated:

> They were all quite nice, but one in particular really caught my attention as having a special charm. He radiated such kindness that people were drawn to him. His name was Pier Giorgio Frassati. For him, religion was always a way of life; it was both light and strength, which illuminated and animated all human activity. He was a man of action, determined to dedicate his philosophy to serving life.[36]

In 1923, Pier Giorgio fell in love with a young woman named Laura Hidalgo. She was a very kind, lovely, and considerate person who deeply treasured her faith. She was a prayerful person who really loved the mountains as much as Pier Giorgio. She was a mathematics major at Turin's Polytechnic University. Pier Giorgio dreamed of making her his wife. His parents were not impressed with her, as they had always dreamed of him marrying a young lady of the upper class. This was the main obstacle to him marrying Laura. His parents' marriage was disintegrating and he just could not bring himself to consider a marriage his parents would oppose, thus putting a strain on a relationship that was already very fragile. He said to Father Antonio Cajazzi, a former teacher: "To destroy one family in order to create another would be absurd and is not even worth thinking about. I will pay the price, but God's will be done."[37] Pier Giorgio wrote a letter to a friend, Isidoro Bonini, and shared his sorrow and pain. In his letter he wrote that only faith could help him in this situation. He asked his friend to please pray for him. As it has been with holy people before Pier Giorgio and will be after him, the brightness, the light that came forth from him seemed to shine brighter in the darkness of the Cross.

In early 1925, Pier Giorgio worked hard to finish his studies at the university so that he could graduate in July. He wanted to be a mining engineer upon graduation, but his father wanted him to be administrative director of the *La Stampa* newspaper, which he founded and directed. In June of 1925, Pier Giorgio started to look thinner and exhausted. He began having migraine headaches and he lost his appetite. The family doctor, Luciano Alvazzi, was called in to examine him and to give a diagnosis. The diagnosis was poliomyelitis, an infectious disease that led to paralysis and a rapid death. A priest was called in to administer the Sacrament of the Sick. On the evening of July 4, 1925, at the age of 24, Pier Giorgio, Mary's "devoted athlete," died silently with a smile on his face and a Rosary in his hand. He was just about to receive his degree in mining engineering at Turin's

Pier Giorgio died on July 4, 1925. He once said, "The day of my death will be the best day of my life." He died with a smile on his face and a Rosary in his hand. On July 6, the funeral was held at the Church of La Crocetta (below), with an overflowing crowd in attendance.

Polytechnic University. He died on a Saturday, a day dedicated to Mary, who always smiled on her cherished athlete in his prayer, service to people, and play. She now smiled on him into eternity.

Pier Giorgio once told his friends, "The day of my death will be the best day of my life." On July 6, the funeral was held at the Church of La Crocetta in Turin, with an overflowing crowd in attendance. A good friend of his wrote on the day of his funeral:

> I have tried to pray, but have not been able to. I began to say a Rosary. But when I saw my hands on the beads that Pier Giorgio gave me not very long ago, his words came back into my head: 'Keep them in memory of me and if every time you say the Rosary you say an extra Hail Mary for me, I'll be very grateful.' Those Rosary beads are and will be the dearest memento I have of him.[38]

After the death of Pier Giorgio, his parents resolved to make their marriage work and his father started to go to Mass again. Pier Giorgio's body was found completely incorrupt upon its exhumation on March 31, 1981. In April 1984, John Paul II called him "model of athletes." His body was transferred in 1990 from the family tomb in Pallone, Italy to the Cathedral of St. John the Baptist in Turin, where today many pilgrims, especially young people, students, and athletes, come to pray at his side. The epitaph on his tomb reads:

> At the age of twenty-four—at the very end of his university career—handsome, strong, good humored, and beloved, he reached unexpectedly his last day on Earth; and as ever, welcomed it serenely as the most beautiful day of his life. The purity of his life and his charitable deeds bear witness to his religious faith. Death transformed him into a living standard held aloft before the eyes of Christian youth.

People from all over the world come to visit Pier Giorgio's tomb, seen here in the Cathedral of John the Baptist in Turin. The young and the old, students, and athletes come to pray at his side.
Oh, Pier Giorgio, please pray for us all!

On May 20, 1990, Pope John Paul II is seen here in St. Peter's Square declaring Pier Giorgio Blessed. *John Paul II called him "the man of the eight beatitudes."*

At the beatification ceremony (above) in St. Peter's Square, John Paul II said of Pier Giorgio: "He left the world rather young, but he made a mark upon our entire century and not only our century."

On May 20, 1990, over 50,000 people gathered in St. Peter's Square to hear John Paul II declare him *Blessed* Pier Giorgio Frassati, "The man of the eight beatitudes." His feast day was established on July 4. John Paul II said of the young Frassati: "He left the world rather young, but he made a mark upon our entire century, and not only our century."[39] On April 6, 1990, on the 100th anniversary of Pier Giorgio's birth, the Polytechnic University of Turin conferred a mining engineering degree to Blessed Pier Giorgio posthumously. Blessed Pier Giorgio will always be remembered for his enthusiasm for the faith, for his life, for his love of the poor, for his devotion to the Rosary, and for his laughter, singing, and cheerfulness.

He is truly an example for young people today. John Paul II had said:

> Pier Giorgio has offered everyone an example that has lost none of its power today. I hope that each of us, especially young people, take from his brief but luminous life the inspiration and incitement to lead a life of coherent Christian witness.[40]

Before leaving the altar on the occasion of his beatification on May 20, 1990, John Paul II stated:

> Dear young people, I invite you to imitate the example of the newly beatified. You too must find a way to devote yourselves often to prayer and meditation, along with the Mother of the Redeemer, in order to rejuvenate your faith and to find inspiration for your service to Christ and the Church in the life example of Mary most holy.[41]

In regard to finding a way to pray and meditate along with Mary in order to rejuvenate your faith and find inspiration as the Pope said, Pier Giorgio would hold up the Rosary to everyone, especially to the young and to athletes, and say "This is the way!"

John Paul II, God's athlete, always taught that the Rosary was his favorite prayer. It was a daily encounter that Mary and he never missed.

4

The Rosary: The Athlete's Prayer

John Paul II, in his homily at a Mass on May 10, 1993, in Caltanissetta, Sicily, talked about how St. Paul compared two types of athletes: athletes of sport and athletes of the faith. The Pope encouraged the young people in attendance to represent both. The athlete of sport uses exercise and nutrition to build up strength for the game on the field. The athlete of the faith uses prayer to build up spiritual strength for the game of life and for achieving the final reward of eternal life with God. Pier Giorgio Frassati would direct everyone, especially athletes, to the Rosary as the prayer to build up our spiritual strength. Many Popes have praised the Rosary as a spiritual training school where people whose muscles of the spirit have grown flabby and atrophied can slowly and normally win back the strength required to come off victoriously in the great battle of life.

The origin of the Rosary is rooted in the thirteenth century. At that time, France was threatened by the Albigensian heresy, which believed that matter was evil and the spirit was good. Their denial of respect for the body was real. They believed that all life on earth—being the work of Satan—was evil. Their anti-life attitude produced a culture of death. In 1208, after much fruitless labor preaching to the Albigensians, the revelation of the Rosary to St. Dominic took place in the Chapel of St. Mary in Prouille, southern France. Dominic was a 36-year-old priest from

Caleruega, Spain. He was a man of great character, with God training him as an athlete of Christ. He is described as being of middle height with a very handsome face and blond hair, with a slightly ruddy complexion. He had a strong voice and radiance came from his head, which attracted many to love and respect him.

St. Dominic was praying and tearfully complaining to Mary, the Mother of God, in the Chapel of St. Mary about the poor fruits of his preaching to the Albigensians. In the midst of his lament, Mary appeared to him and said:

> Wonder not that until now you have obtained so little fruit by your labors: You have spent them on a barren soil, not yet watered with the dew of divine grace. When God willed to renew the face of the earth, He began by sending down on it the fertilizing rain of the Angelic Salutation. Preach my Psalter (Rosary) composed of 150 Angelic Salutations and 15 Our Fathers and you will obtain an abundant harvest.[42]

Mary taught Dominic this method of praying and ordered him to preach it far and wide. It is said of Dominic that he would go from town to town and teach the Rosary. He established the *Confraternity of the Rosary* in nearly every town he preached in.

In his travels he showed tremendous physical endurance. His contemporaries described him as the "strong athlete," always commenting on his vigorous nature. His slim figure retained its youthfulness and flexibility under all the physical efforts of travel. He would preach on the Gospel truths that centered on the joyful, sorrowful, and glorious life of Christ. He would invite his hearers to pick up the string of knots or beads and pray the Our Father and Hail Mary only after he gave a sermon on a particular mystery, a phase of Jesus' life. St. Dominic has the honor of being the author

The revelation of the Rosary was given to St. Dominic in Prouille. This basilica in Prouille is in honor of Our Lady of the Rosary. Pius XI stated: "Prouille was the cradle of the Rosary."

*God trained St. Dominic to be an **athlete of Christ**.
Mary taught him the method of praying the Rosary
and ordered him to preach it far and wide.*

of the Rosary, though he did not compose it in the definitive form
we have today. The fixing of definite mysteries was a long process
that took centuries to evolve and determine. This was done by St.
Pius V in 1569. This Dominican Pope set into place the joyful,
sorrowful, and glorious mysteries. On October 16, 2002, John
Paul II made an addition to the traditional 15 mysteries. These
new mysteries are called "mysteries of light" (see pg. 101).
They include the mysteries of Jesus' public ministry between his
Baptism and his Passion.

St. Dominic loved the company of the young. The character of St. Dominic and his outlook on life drew the young to him.
Dominic had playfulness in his character and yearly grew more
boyish, more light of heart. He believed in the young and their
potential to do great things for God and climb instantly to places
of importance. He was always affectionate to everyone and very
good to talk to when in trouble. He always made people feel
at home when talking to him. In 1213 the battle of Muret, in
southern France near Toulouse, played a part in St. Dominic's life.
It was a battle between the Catholic soldiers and the Albigensian
soldiers. The Catholics were greatly outnumbered. Dominic suggested that the Rosary be prayed before the battle. During the
battle, Dominic prayed the Rosary in the Church of St. James with
his arms extended. The Catholic soldiers attributed their victory to
the Rosary. In gratitude, Simon de Montfort built the first chapel
in honor of the Rosary, located in the Church of St. James, not
far from Toulouse.

Dominic was like David of old, using his Rosary as a
slingshot, a weapon against evil. He was like a doctor, using the
Rosary as a serum, injecting all the afflicted with it so that vices
would be rooted out and virtues infused. The Rosary was like
an ointment that St. Dominic and his followers used to heal
the members of both Church and State. Throughout his life, St.

Dominic had nothing more at heart than to praise Mary and to inspire everyone to honor her by praying the Rosary. This "holy athlete" and a "true light of the world" died on August 6, 1221 at the age of 51. After his death, Dominicans throughout the centuries, like Pier Giorgio Frassati, have followed the example of St. Dominic by using the Rosary in fighting the "isms" of their day, which like the Albigensian heresy of Dominic's time are contrary to the teachings of the Church. In his apostolic letter on the Rosary (see appendix), John Paul II stated:

> The history of the Rosary shows how this prayer was used in particular by the Dominicans at a difficult time for the Church, due to the spread of heresy. Today we are facing new challenges. Why should we not once more have recourse to the Rosary, with the same faith as those who have gone before us (n. 17).

If you would like to read more of the life of St. Dominic and the Rosary, see the author's book *The Rosary: The Little Summa* (Aquinas Press).

In the 1560s Turkish forces threatened Europe, and Sultan Selim II wanted to take the cross down from atop St. Peter's in Rome, to replace it with a crescent. Pope St. Pius V asked all Catholics to pray the Rosary for success in stopping the advances of the Moslems. In 1571, there was a great battle of Lepanto off the coast of Nafpaktos, Greece in the Gulf of Corinth. The Catholic fleet was greatly outnumbered. Pope St. Pius V launched a crusade of prayer. He asked that the Rosary be prayed. All the members of the Catholic fleet prayed the Rosary before the battle. On October 7, 1571, the Pope stood up at four o'clock in the afternoon during a conclave of cardinals and gazed out the window, finally turning around to the cardinals, his face glowing with a strange light, and announced: "This is no time for business.

In 1571, the great battle of Lepanto was fought here off the coast of Nafpaktos, Greece in the Gulf of Corinth (above). A monument is seen here (below) commemorating this battle.

Go and thank God. Our fleet has just won the victory." Pope St. Pius V attributed the victory to the Rosary. The Venetian Senate wrote: "It was not generals nor battalions nor arms that brought us victory; but it was Our Lady of the Rosary."

Mary appeared in Fatima, Portugal in 1917 to three children. She called herself the Lady of the Rosary. She appeared to Jacinta, age seven; Francisco, her brother, age nine; and Lucia, their cousin, age 10. She appeared to them on six occasions from May 13, 1917 to October 13, 1917. On October 13, 1917, she said: "I am the Lady of the Rosary. I want a chapel built here in my honor. Continue to pray the Rosary every day."[43] In his apostolic letter on the Rosary (see appendix), John Paul II mentioned Fatima as an occasion in which Mary made her presence felt and her voice heard, in order to exhort us to this form of contemplative prayer. In each of the six apparitions, Mary urged with great insistence that we pray the Rosary every day. In his apostolic letter on the Rosary, John Paul II stated:

> The Church has always attributed particular efficacy to this prayer, entrusting to the Rosary the most difficult problems. At times when Christianity itself seemed under threat, its deliverance was attributed to the power of this prayer, and Our Lady of the Rosary was acclaimed as the one whose intercession brought salvation (n. 39).

Jacinta, the youngest of the children, was questioned and asked what was the chief thing Mary had told Lucia. Her reply was: "That we should pray the Rosary every day." Lucia became Sister Lucia and lived for many years as a Carmelite nun in a Carmelite convent in Coimbra, Portugal. She died on February 13, 2005 at the age of 97. She was an extraordinary and special person, of whom John Paul II wrote: "I always felt supported by the daily gift of her prayers, especially in difficult moments of trial and

Mary came to Fatima in 1917 and appeared to these three children: Jacinta (age seven), Francisco (age nine), and Lucia (age 10). Mary appeared to them between May 13, 1917 and October 13, 1917.

suffering. May the Lord repay her abundantly for the great service she gave the Church." Sister Lucia had analyzed Mary's message and has shared it with us. In her book *Calls from the Message of Fatima*, she states:

> "All well-intentioned people can and should recite the five decades of the Rosary every day. The Rosary should constitute each person's spiritual food. We must pray the Rosary every day, because we need to pray and we must do so."[44]

In her book she also states:

> "God, who is our Father and understands better than we do the needs of His children, chose to stoop to the simple, ordinary level of all of us in asking for the daily recitation of the Rosary, in order to smooth for us the way to him."

In regard to Mary's September 13, 1917 request, *"Continue to pray the Rosary in order to obtain the end of the war,"* Sister Lucia in her book makes the following comment:

> Clearly, at the time, the Message was referring to the first World War, which was afflicting so many people just then. But the word war also stands for all other wars going on all around us and which we must help to bring to an end by our prayer and self-sacrifice. I think, too, of the wars waged against us by the enemies of our eternal salvation: the devil, the world, and our own carnal nature.[45]

Mary revealed a three-part secret to Lucia and her cousins on July 13, 1917. The first two consisted of a vision of hell and devotion to the Immaculate Heart of Mary. The third part consisted of an attack on the Pope in the future, which turned out to be John Paul II. If you would like to know more about the Rosary, devotion

Sister Lucia, seen here with John Paul II at Fatima, states that "all well-intentioned people can, and should, recite the five decades of the Rosary every day. The Rosary should constitute each person's spiritual food."

to the Immaculate Heart of Mary, and the third part of the secret, you can read about it in the author's book *The Rosary: The Little Summa.*

On October 16, 2002 in St. Peter's Square, John Paul II signed his apostolic letter *The Rosary of the Virgin Mary* (see appendix), which presents the Rosary as an outstanding way to contemplate the face and mysteries of Christ. The Pope stated in his Rosary letter: "With the Rosary, the Christian people sits at the School of Mary and is led to contemplate the beauty on the face of Christ and to experience the depths of his love" (n. 1). This marvelous papal document will help people rediscover the mystical depth contained in the simplicity of the Rosary. This apostolic letter on the Rosary is highly recommended reading for everyone.

John Paul II in his apostolic letter *For the New Millennium* mentioned that the contemplation of the mystery of Jesus is genuine "training in holiness." What better way for the athlete to train for this than praying the Rosary and contemplating the mystery of Jesus, like our mother Mary did. The Pope wrote in this apostolic letter: "Together, we must all imitate the contemplation of Mary, who returned home to Nazareth from her pilgrimage to the Holy City of Jerusalem treasuring in her heart the mystery of her son" (Lk 2:51).

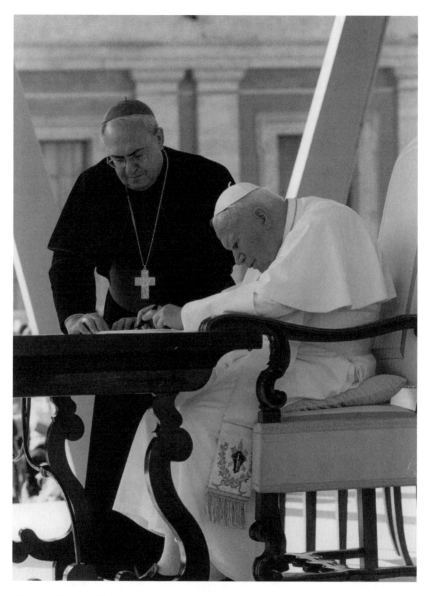

John Paul II is seen here signing his apostolic letter on the Rosary in St. Peter's Square on October 16, 2002. In it, he presents the Rosary as an outstanding way to contemplate the face and mysteries of Christ. He called the Rosary "The School of Mary."

HOW TO PRAY THE ROSARY

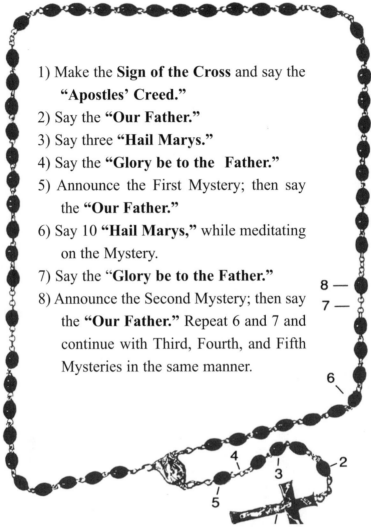

1) Make the **Sign of the Cross** and say the "**Apostles' Creed.**"
2) Say the "**Our Father.**"
3) Say three "**Hail Marys.**"
4) Say the "**Glory be to the Father.**"
5) Announce the First Mystery; then say the "**Our Father.**"
6) Say 10 "**Hail Marys,**" while meditating on the Mystery.
7) Say the "**Glory be to the Father.**"
8) Announce the Second Mystery; then say the "**Our Father.**" Repeat 6 and 7 and continue with Third, Fourth, and Fifth Mysteries in the same manner.

After each decade say the following prayer requested by the Blessed Virgin Mary at Fatima: "O my Jesus, forgive us our sins, save us from the fires of hell, lead all souls to heaven, especially those who have most need of your mercy."

Say the **Hail, Holy Queen** after the five decades are completed.

Say an **Our Father**, **Hail Mary**, and **Glory be** for the Pope's intentions at the end.

The following suggestions of John Paul II and the author can be very helpful in praying the Rosary:

1) Before praying the Rosary, ask Mary to help you meditate with her on the mysteries of the Rosary. You can say the introductory prayer the Pope mentioned in his Rosary letter: *"O God, come to my aid; O Lord make haste to help me.'* In some places it is customary to begin with the opening words of Psalm 70, as if to nourish in those who are praying a humble awareness of their own insufficiency" (n. 37).

2) Meditate on each mystery before you pray the Our Father and Hail Mary. The short meditations which start on pg. 102 will be most helpful in meditating on each mystery. In his Rosary letter, the Pope wrote that after the announcement of the mystery, he suggests meditation on a Biblical passage, long or short, that has to pertain to the mystery announced. He also recommends that after the meditation, a moment of silence be given for the mind to focus on the content of the mystery. The Pope stressed the contemplative or meditative dimension of the Rosary in his apostolic letter. He stated: "Without contemplation, the Rosary is a body without a soul, and its recitation runs the risk of becoming a mechanical repetition of formulas" (n. 12). He continually called the Rosary a contemplative prayer and " a compendium of the Gospel."

3) Ask of God, through Mary, for a virtue that shines in the life of Jesus and Mary in each mystery, or one that you are in need of. Virtues to be prayed for in each mystery can be found on pg. 101.

4) In praying the Our Father and Hail Mary, do so with reverence; that is, slowly and with attention. Pope Paul VI recommended a quiet rhythm and a lingering pace. St. Albert the Great, a Dominican, advised people to greet Mary in the same way you would like her to greet you. John

Paul II recommended the custom of mentioning the name of Jesus in the Hail Mary, followed by the addition of a clause referring to the mystery. The Pope stated that using clauses after the name of Jesus is praiseworthy. The Pope saw the clauses as an aid in concentrating our meditation. The following clauses said after the name Jesus can be helpful:

First Joyful Mystery	Jesus, incarnate
Second Joyful Mystery	Jesus, sanctifying
Third Joyful Mystery	Jesus, born in poverty
Fourth Joyful Mystery	Jesus, sacrificed
Fifth Joyful Mystery	Jesus, Saint among saints
First Luminous Mystery	Jesus, the beloved Son of the Father
Second Luminous Mystery	Jesus, changing water into wine or Jesus, manifesting his glory
Third Luminous Mystery	Jesus, proclaiming the coming of the kingdom of God *or* Jesus, calling to conversion and forgiving sin
Fouth Luminous Mystery	Jesus, whose face shines forth the glory of the Godhead
Fifth Luminous Mystery	Jesus, the bread of life *or* Jesus, offering his Body and Blood as food
First Sorrowful Mystery	Jesus, in His agony
Second Sorrowful Mystery	Jesus, scourged
Third Sorrowful Mystery	Jesus, crowned with thorns
Fourth Sorrowful Mystery	Jesus, carrying His cross
Fifth Sorrowful Mystery	Jesus, crucified

First Glorious Mystery	Jesus, risen from the dead
Second Glorious Mystery	Jesus, ascending to heaven
Third Glorious Mystery	Jesus, filling Mary with the Holy Spirit
Fourth Glorious Mystery	Jesus, raising Mary up
Fifth Glorious Mystery	Jesus, crowning Mary

5) The Pope recommends that the Glory Be prayer at the end of each decade be given importance. He suggests it be sung in public recitation. John Paul II taught us that the glorification of the Trinity at the end of each decade raises the mind to the heights of heaven.

6) The Pope welcomed us to pray for the Pope and his intentions, embracing all the needs of the Church. He taught us that the Church grants indulgences to those who pray the Rosary with the required disposition. We can say an Our Father, Hail Mary, and Glory Be for the Pope's intentions at the end of the Rosary.

7) John Paul II invited us to conclude the Rosary with the Hail Holy Queen prayer (see pg. 97) or the Litany of Loreto (see pg. 98). The Pope mentioned that either prayer is the crowning moment of an inner journey which has brought the faithful into living contact with the mystery of Christ and Mary.

8) John Paul II encouraged us to pray the Rosary properly; otherwise there is a risk that the Rosary will fail to produce the intended spiritual effects. In his Rosary letter, John Paul II stated that if prayed properly, the Rosary will truly become a spiritual itinerary in which Mary acts as Mother, Teacher, and Guide, sustaining the faithful by her powerful intercession.

9) We are to pray the Rosary with perseverance. St. Louis de Montfort taught that we must continue to pray the Rosary when we experience in

prayer such things as dryness of soul, distraction, boredom, discouragement, and distress.

10) John Paul II had suggested a certain day for each of the mysteries of the Rosary:

On Monday and Saturday—The Joyful Mysteries
On Tuesday and Friday—The Sorrowful Mysteries
On Wednesday and Sunday—The Glorious
　　Mysteries
On Thursday—The Mysteries of Light.

John Paul II had requested that the young be taught the Rosary. In his Rosary letter, he stated: "If the Rosary is well presented, I am sure that young people will once more surprise adults by the way they make this prayer their own and recite it with the enthusiasm typical of their age group" (n. 42). The Confraternity of the Rosary is a beneficial association to consider being a member of. Pier Giorgio Frassati became a member when he was 17 years old. The Confraternity was originated in the thirteenth century by St. Dominic. He established it in nearly every town he preached the Rosary. Ecclesiastical writers have called the Confraternity of the Rosary "the praying army enrolled by St. Dominic under the banner of the Mother of God."

Mary has promised in her well-known Rosary promises: "I have obtained from my Son that all members of the Confraternity of the Rosary shall have in life and in death all the Blessed in Heaven as their intercessors." St. John Vianney said: "If anyone has the happiness of being in the Confraternity of the Holy Rosary, he and she have in all corners of the globe brothers and sisters who pray for them." The Dominican Order admits all members of the Confraternity to share in the Masses, Rosaries, apostolic work, prayers, and penances of all the members of the Dominican family throughout the world. The only obligation (which does not bind under sin) imposed on the members is to recite during the course of each week three five-decade Rosaries, which would include and cover all the 15 traditional mysteries of the Rosary. All members pray for one another and for the intentions of one another. If you wish to be a member of the Confraternity of the Rosary, send your full name and address to:

Rosary Center, Dominican Fathers
P.O. Box 3617
Portland, Oregon 97208.

Promises of Our Lady to those who Devoutly Pray the Rosary

1.) Whoever shall faithfully serve me by the recitation of the Rosary shall receive signal graces.

2.) I promise my special protection and the greatest graces to all those who shall recite the Rosary.

3.) The Rosary shall be a powerful armour against hell; it will destroy vice, decrease sin, and defeat heresies.

4.) It will cause virtue and good works to flourish; it will obtain for souls the abundant mercy of God; it will withdraw the hearts of men from the love of the world and its vanities; and will lift them to the desire of eternal things. Oh, that souls would sanctify themselves by this means.

5.) The soul which recommends itself to me by the recitation of the Rosary shall not perish.

6.) Whoever shall recite the Rosary devoutly, applying himself to the consideration of its sacred mysteries, shall never be conquered by misfortune. God will not chastise him in His justice, he shall not perish by an unprovided death; if he be just he shall remain in the grace of God, and become worthy of eternal life.

7.) Whoever shall have a true devotion for the Rosary shall not die without the sacraments of the Church.

8.) Those who are faithful to recite the Rosary shall have during their life and at their death the light of God and the plenitude of His graces; at the moment of death they shall participate in the merits of the saints in paradise.

9.) I will deliver very promptly from purgatory those who have been devoted to the Rosary.

10.) The faithful children of the Rosary shall merit a high degree of glory in heaven.

11.) You shall obtain all you ask of me by the recitation of the Rosary.

12.) All those who propagate the Holy Rosary shall be aided by me in all their necessities.

13.) I have obtained from my Divine Son that all the advocates of the Rosary shall have for intercessors the entire celestial court during their life and at the hour of their death.

14.) All who recite the Rosary are all my beloved children, the brothers and sisters of Jesus Christ.

15.) Devotion to my Rosary is a great sign of predestination. (Given to St. Dominic and Alan de la Roche, O.P.)

Prayers of the Rosary

The Sign of the Cross

In the name of the Father, and of the Son, and of the Holy Spirit. *Amen.*

The Apostles' Creed

I believe in God, the Father Almighty, Creator of heaven and earth; and in Jesus Christ, his only Son, Our Lord, who was conceived by the Holy Spirit, born of the Virgin Mary, suffered under Pontius Pilate, was crucified, died, and was buried. He descended into hell; the third day He rose again from the dead.

He ascended into heaven, and is seated at the right hand of God, the Father almighty. From thence He shall come to judge the living and the dead. I believe in the Holy Spirit, the Holy Catholic Church, the Communion of Saints, the forgiveness of sins, the resurrection of the body, and life everlasting. *Amen.*

The Our Father

Our Father who art in heaven, hallowed be thy Name. Thy Kingdom come, Thy will be done on earth as it is in heaven. Give us this day our daily bread, and forgive us our trespasses, as we forgive those who trespass against us, and lead us not into temptation, but deliver us from evil. *Amen.*

The Hail Mary

Hail Mary, full of grace, the Lord is with thee; blessed art thou among women, and blessed is the fruit of thy womb, Jesus. Holy Mary, Mother of God, pray for us sinners, now and at the hour of our death. *Amen.*

The Glory be to the Father

Glory be to the Father, and to the Son, and to the Holy Spirit. As it was in the beginning, is now, and ever shall be, world without end. *Amen.*

The Hail, Holy Queen

Hail, Holy Queen, Mother of Mercy, our life, our sweetness, and our hope! To thee do we cry, poor banished children of Eve! To thee do we send up our sighs, mourning and weeping in this valley of tears. Turn then, most gracious advocate, thine eyes of mercy towards us; and after this, our exile, show unto us the blessed fruit of thy womb, Jesus! O clement, O loving, O sweet Virgin Mary! Pray for us, O holy Mother of God, that we may be made worthy of the promises of Christ.

Litany of Loreto

Lord, have mercy.

Christ, have mercy.

Lord, have mercy.

Christ, hear us.

Christ, graciously hear us.

God, the Father of heaven, have mercy on us.

God the Son, Redeemer of the world, have mercy on us.

God the Holy Spirit, have mercy on us.

Holy Trinity, one God, have mercy on us.

Holy Mary, pray for us.

Holy Mother of God, pray for us.

Holy Virgin of Virgins, pray for us.

Mother of Christ, pray for us.

Mother of the Church, pray for us.

Mother of divine grace, pray for us.

Mother most pure, pray for us.

Mother most chaste, pray for us.

Mother inviolate, pray for us.

Mother undefiled, pray for us.

Mother most amiable, pray for us.

Mother of good counsel, pray for us.

Mother of our Creator, pray for us.

Mother of our Savior, pray for us.

Virgin most prudent, pray for us

Virgin most venerable, pray for us.

Virgin most renowned, pray for us.

Virgin most powerful, pray for us.

Virgin most merciful, pray for us.

Virgin most faithful, pray for us.

Mirror of justice, pray for us.

Seat of wisdom, pray for us.

Cause of our joy, pray for us.

Vessel of honor, pray for us.

Singular vessel of devotion, pray for us.

Mystical rose, pray for us.

Tower of David, pray for us.

Tower of ivory, pray for us.

Tower of gold, pray for us.

Ark of the covenant, pray for us.

Gate of heaven, pray for us.

Morning star, pray for us.

Health of the sick, pray for us.

Refuge of sinners, pray for us.

Comforter of the afflicted, pray for us.

Help of Christians, pray for us.

Queen of angels, pray for us.

Queen of patriarchs, pray for us.

Queen of prophets, pray for us.

Queen of apostles, pray for us.

Queen of martyrs, pray for us.

Queen of confessors, pray for us.

Queen of virgins, pray for us.

Queen of all saints, pray for us.

Queen conceived without original sin, pray for us.

Queen assumed into heaven, pray for us.

Queen of the most holy Rosary, pray for us.

Queen of the family, pray for us.

Queen of peace, pray for us.

Lamb of God, who takest away the sins of the world, spare us,
O Lord.

Lamb of God, who takest away the sins of the world, graciously
hear us, O Lord.

Lamb of God, who takest away the sins of the world, have mercy on us.

V. Pray for us, O holy Mother of God.
R. That we may be made worthy of the promises of Christ.

Let us pray:
Grant, we beseech Thee, O Lord God, that your servants may enjoy lasting health of mind and body, and by the glorious intercession of the Blessed Mary, ever Virgin, be delivered from present sorrow and enter into the joy of eternal happiness. Through Christ our Lord.

R. *Amen.*

The Mysteries of the Rosary

Joyful Mysteries: Monday and Saturday

Virtue or gift to be prayed for:

1.) The Annunciation - Faith
2.) The Visitation - Charity
3.) The Birth of Jesus - Humility
4.) The Presentation of Jesus in the Temple - Self-Giving
5.) The Finding of the Child Jesus in the Temple - Wisdom

Mysteries of Light: Thursday

1.) The Baptism of the Lord - Awareness of our dignity as children of God
2.) The Wedding Feast at Cana - Trust in God's providence
3.) The Proclamation of the Kingdom - To be a light to the world
4.) The Transfiguration - To adore Jesus in the Eucharist
5.) The Institution of the Eucharist - Great faith in the Eucharist

Sorrowful Mysteries: Tuesday and Friday

1.) The Agony in the Garden - Perseverence in prayer
2.) The Scourging at the Pillar - Chastity
3.) The Crowning with Thorns - Contrition and repentance
4.) The Carrying of the Cross - Fortitude
5.) The Crucifixion - Being open to God's mercy and forgiveness

Glorious Mysteries: Wednesday and Sunday

1.) The Resurrection of Jesus - Hope
2.) The Ascension of Jesus into Heaven - Desire for Heaven
3.) The Descent of the Holy Spirit - Gifts of the Holy Spirit
4.) The Assumption of Mary into Heaven - Love for Mary as our Mother
5.) The Coronation of Mary - Devotion to her Rosary

Short Meditations

The Five Joyful Mysteries:

1.) The Annunciation

1.) The time for the incarnation is at hand.

2.) Of all women, God prepared Mary from her conception to be the Mother of the Incarnate Word.

3.) The Angel Gabriel announces, "Hail, full of grace! The Lord is with thee."

4.) Mary wonders at this salutation.

5.) The Angel assures her: "Fear not . . . you shall conceive in your womb, and give birth to a Son."

6.) Mary is troubled, for she has made a vow of virginity.

7.) The Angel answers that she will conceive by the power of the Holy Spirit, and her Son will be called the Son of God.

8.) The Incarnation awaits Mary's consent.

9.) Mary answers: "Behold the handmaid of the Lord. Be it done unto me according to your word."

10.) The Word was made flesh and dwelt amongst us.

2.) The Visitation

1.) Mary's cousin Elizabeth conceived a son in her old age, for nothing is impossible with God.

2.) Charity prompts Mary to hasten to visit Elizabeth in the hour of her need.

3.) The journey to Elizabeth's home is about eighty miles, requiring four or five days.

4.) Though long and arduous, the journey is joyous, for Mary bears with her the Incarnate Word.

5.) At Mary's salutation, John the Baptist is sanctified in his mother's womb.

6.) Elizabeth exclaims: "Blessed are you among women, and blessed is the fruit of your womb."

7.) "How have I deserved that the mother of my Lord should come to me?"

8.) "Blessed is she who believed that the Lord's words to her would be fulfilled."

9.) Mary replies: "My soul proclaims the greatness of the Lord, and my spirit finds joy in God my Savior."

10.) Mary serves her cousin in all humility for three months until the birth of John the Baptist.

3.) The Nativity

1.) Joseph and Mary go to Bethlehem to comply with the decree of Caesar Augustus.

2.) The hour for Mary to give birth is near, but there is no room in the inn.

3.) In the stillness of the night, the Savior is born in a cave, Mary remaining a Virgin.

4.) She wraps Him in swaddling clothes and lays Him in a manger.

5.) In unspeakable joy Mary gathers to her bosom the Flower of her virginity.

6.) Jesus enters the world in poverty to teach the lesson of detachment from earthly things.

7.) The angel announces to the shepherds: "Today there is born to you in the town of David a Savior, Who is Christ the Lord."

8.) The angelic chorus sings: "Glory to God in the highest, and peace to His people on earth."

9.) The shepherds come to the stable to pay homage to the infant Jesus.

10.) The Magi come to adore the Holy Child and offer Him gifts.

4.) The Presentation of Jesus in the Temple

1.) Observing the law of Moses they take Jesus to the temple to present Him to the Lord.

2.) According to the Law the firstborn male child of every family should be consecrated to the Lord.

3.) Mary offers her Son to the Father, then ransoms Him back at the price paid by the poor.

4.) Jesus is not subject to the law of Moses, yet to teach obedience, submits to it.

5.) Mary is not subject to the law of purification, yet in humility she submits to it.

6.) God had revealed to Simeon that he would not see death until he had seen the Messiah.

7.) Recognizing the Child, he prays: "Now you can dismiss your servant in peace. You have fulfilled your word."

8.) "This Child is destined to be the downfall and rise of many in Israel, a sign that will be opposed."

9.) And to Mary, Simeon reveals: "And your own soul a sword shall pierce."

10.) After they fulfill all the Law requires, they return to Nazareth.

5.) The Finding of the Child Jesus in the Temple

1.) When Jesus is 12 years old, He goes with His parents to Jerusalem for the feast of the Passover.

2.) After the feast of the Passover, Joseph and Mary unknowingly set out for Nazareth without Jesus.

3.) At the end of the first day's journey they discover Jesus is missing.

4.) His parents return immediately, looking for Him.

5.) This loss causes grief and anxiety beyond our understanding to the hearts of Mary and Joseph.

6.) On the third day they find Jesus in the Temple among the

Doctors, who were astonished at His wisdom.

7.) Mary: "Son, why have you done this to us? Your father and I have been searching for you in sorrow."

8.) Jesus: "Why did you search for me? Did you not know that I must be about my Father's business?"

9.) Jesus goes down with them to Nazareth, and is subject to them.

10.) Mary keeps all these things in her heart.

The Five Mysteries of Light:

1.) The Baptism of the Lord

1.) John the Baptist was sent from God to testify to the light. He preaches at the Jordan River a baptism of repentance for the forgiveness of sins.

2.) Jesus begins his public life after being baptized by St. John the Baptist in the Jordan River.

3.) When Jesus had been baptized and was praying - the heaven was opened.

4.) The Holy Spirit descended in bodily form as a dove and the Father said: Thou art my beloved son, with whom I am well pleased.

5.) Jesus' prayer after his Baptism teaches that after Baptism man needs to pray continually in order to enter heaven.

6.) The Fathers of the Church taught that Christ was baptized to sanctify the waters that they might be used for the cleaning from sin in Christian baptism.

7.) The dove came down upon Jesus to show that the Holy Spirit would come invisibly to the soul through baptism.

8.) The Baptism in the Jordan is first of all a mystery of light. Christ descends into the waters, the innocent one who became "sin" for our sake.

9.) The presence of all three divine Persons at the baptism of Jesus show: Go and teach all nations, baptize them in the name of the Father, Son, and Holy Spirit.

10.) God anointed Jesus of Nazareth with the Holy Spirit and with power, that he might be revealed to Israel as its Messsiah.

2.) The Marriage Feast at Cana

1.) There was a marriage at Cana in Galilee and the Mother of Jesus was there. Jesus was also invited with his disciples.

2.) The hosts ran out of wine. Mary noticed it and said to Jesus: "They have no wine."

3.) Jesus said: "What is that to me and to you; my hour has not yet come."

4.) Mary said to the servants: "Do whatever he tells you."

5.) Six jars were sitting there, each holding 20 or 30 gallons. Jesus said to the servants: "Fill the jars with water." And they filled them up to the brim.

6.) Jesus said: "Now draw some out, and take it to the steward of the feast."

7.) Then the steward tasted the water, now wine, and said to the bridegroom" Every man serves the good wine first, then the poor wine, but you have kept the good wine until now."

8.) This was the first of Jesus' signs and it manifested his glory.

9.) Seeing this miracle, the disciples believed in him.

10.) Christ changes water into wine and opens the hearts of the disciples to faith, thanks to the intervention of Mary.

3.) The Proclamation of the Kingdom of God

1.) After John the Baptist was arrested, Jesus came into Galilee and said: "The time is fulfilled and the kingdom of God is at hand: repent and believe in the Gospel."

2.) To carry out the will of the Father, Jesus started the kingdom of heaven on earth (the Church). Everyone is called to enter the Kingdom.

3.) It is the will of the Father to raise up men to share in his own divine life. He does this by gathering men around his Son Jesus Christ.

4.) This gathering is the Church, on earth the seed and beginning of that kingdom.

5.) To become a child in relation to God is the condition for entering the Kingdom. For this, we must humble ourselves and become little.

6.) Jesus invites sinners to the kingdom: "I came not to call the righteous, but sinners."

7.) Jesus forgives the sins of all who draw near to him in humble trust.

8.) Jesus starting the ministry of mercy, which he continues to exercise until the end of the world, particularly through the Sacrament of Penance.

9.) Jesus has entrusted the Sacrament of Penance to his Church. Jesus came to free men from the greatest slavery, sin.

10.) Jesus reveals his Father "rich in mercy" and the joy in heaven over one sinner who repents.

4.) The Transfiguration

1.) The Transfiguration takes place on a high mountain (Mt. Tabor). Peter, James, and John are witnesses.

2.) The glory of the Godhead shines forth from the face of Christ. His clothes become dazzling with light.

3.) Moses and Elijah appear on the mountain, speaking of his departure, which Jesus was to accomplish at Jerusalem.

4.) Peter and the two others said: Master, it is good we are here. They appear entranced by the beauty of the Redeemer. This can be seen as an icon of Christian contemplation.

5.) A cloud covers them and a voice from heaven says: "This is my Son, my Chosen; listen to him."

6.) The Father commands the astonished Apostles to listen to him and to prepare to experience with him the agony of the passion.

7.) The Father wishes the Apostles to come with Jesus to the joy of the Resurrection and a life transfigured by the Holy Spirit.

8.) Jesus' Transfiguration aims at strengthening the Apostles' faith in anticipation of his Passion.

9.) The ascent onto the high mountain prepares for the ascent to Calvary.

10.) The Transfiguration gives us a foretaste of Christ's glorious coming. He will change our lowly body to be like his glorious body.

5.) The Institution of the Eucharist

1.) Shortly after the miracle of the loaves and fishes, Jesus in the synagogue in Capernaum said, "I am the bread of life that has come down from heaven."

2.) "If anyone eat of this bread, he shall live forever and the bread I give is my flesh for the life of the world."

3.) "He who eats my flesh and drinks my blood has life everlasting and I will raise him up on the last day."

4.) "For my flesh is food indeed and my blood is drink indeed."

5.) "I am the bread of life; he who comes to me shall not hunger, and he who believes in me shall never thirst."

6.) Some months after his sermon in Capernaum, Jesus, at the Last Supper, instituted the Eucharistic sacrifice of his Body and Blood to fulfill what he had announced at Capernaum.

7.) Jesus took bread, blessed and broke it, and giving it to the disciples, said: "Take and eat it; this is my body."

8.) Taking a cup, he gave thanks and gave it to them saying: "All of you drink of this, for this is my blood of the new covenant, which is being shed for many unto the forgiveness of sins. Do this in remembrance of me."

9.) The Eucharist is thus a sacrifice because it represents (makes present) the sacrifice of the cross.

10.) The Eucharist is the "source and summit of the Christian life. Communion with the Body and Blood of Christ increases the person's union with Jesus, forgives his venial sins, and preserves him from grave sins."

The Five Sorrowful Mysteries:

1.) The Agony in the Garden

1.) Jesus comes with his disciples to Gethsemani: "Stay here while I go yonder and pray."

2.) Entering the garden with Peter, James, and John, Jesus prays, "My soul is sorrowful unto death."

3.) Jesus sees the sins of all mankind, whose guilt He has taken upon Himself.

4.) He sees the wrath of the Father which His sufferings must appease.

5.) So great is His anguish that His sweat becomes as drops of blood falling to the ground.

6.) An angel appears to Him from heaven to strengthen Him.

7.) "Father, if it be possible, let this cup pass from Me; yet, not My will but Yours be done."

8.) Finding the disciples asleep: "Could you not watch one hour with me?"

9.) Jesus is betrayed by Judas, cruelly bound and led away.

10.) Father, by the merits of the agony of Jesus in the Garden, have mercy on us and on the whole world.

2.) The Scourging at the Pillar

1.) Jesus is taken before the High Priest, where He is falsely accused, buffeted, and insulted.

2.) The Jewish leaders take Jesus before Pilate, for only he can impose the death penalty.

3.) The robber Barabbas is preferred to Jesus.

4.) Pilate can "find no cause in Him," yet to appease the Jews, he offers Jesus to be scourged.

5.) The scourge is made of leather thongs to which are attached small sharp bones.

6.) Jesus is bound to a pillar and cruelly scourged until His whole body is covered with deep wounds.

7.) The Lamb of God offers His suffering for the sins of mankind.

8.) Jesus suffers so much in His sacred flesh to satisfy, especially, for sins of the flesh.

9.) The prophecy of Isaiah is fulfilled: "He was wounded for our iniquities, He was bruised for our sins."

10.) Father, by the merits of Jesus in this painful scourging, have mercy on us and on the whole world.

3.) The Crowning with Thorns

1.) Pilate asks: "Are You a king?" Jesus answers: "I am a King, but My kingdom is not of this world."

2.) In the praetorium, the soldiers place an old purple robe on Jesus in mockery of His claim to be a king.

3.) They fashion a crown out of thorns and forcefully press it down upon His head.

4.) In His bound hands they place a reed, as a scepter, in mockery of His kingship.

5.) Kneeling before Him in derision, they spit on Him and cry out, "Hail, King of the Jews!"

6.) Taking the reed from His hand, they strike Him on the head, driving the thorns more deeply into His scalp.

7.) Pilate brings Jesus before the people, hoping His pitiful sight will soften them: Behold the man!"

8.) Their response: "Crucify Him! Crucify Him!"

9.) Our Blessed Lord submitted to this terrible humiliation to make reparation for our pride.

10.) Father, by the merits of this painful humiliation, have mercy on us and on the whole world.

4.) The Carrying of the Cross

1.) One condemned to death by crucifixion is forced to carry the cross to the place of execution.

2.) The suffering of Jesus is intense as the cross is laid on His bruised and wounded back and shoulders.

3.) Weak and exhausted from loss of blood, lack of food and rest, Jesus falls three times under the cross.

4.) Jesus meets His afflicted Mother, causing untold anguish in the hearts of Son and Mother.

5.) The countenance of Jesus is disfigured with blood and sweat, with dust and spittle.

6.) Veronica wipes His face, leaving on her towel the image of His countenance.

7.) Fearing that Jesus might die on the way, the soldiers force Simon of Cyrene to carry the cross behind Jesus.

8.) Jesus speaks to weeping women: "Weep not for Me, but for yourselves and your children."

9.) "If anyone is to be My disciple, let him take up his cross and follow Me."

10.) Father, by the merits of this painful journey to Calvary. Have mercy on us and on the whole world.

5.) The Crucifixion

1.) The hands and feet of Jesus are nailed to the cross in the presence of His afflicted Mother.

2.) "Father, forgive them, for they know not what they do."

3.) "This day you will be with Me in paradise."

4.) "Woman, behold your Son. Son, behold your Mother."

5.) "My God, My God, why have You forsaken Me?"

6.) "I thirst."

7.) "It is finished."

8.) "Father, into Your hands I commend My spirit."

9.) The side of Jesus is pierced with a lance. His body is taken down and placed in the arms of His Mother.

10.) Father, by the merits of the crucifixion and death of Jesus, have mercy on us and on the whole world.

The Five Glorious Mysteries

1.) The Resurrection of Jesus

1.) The body of Jesus is placed in the tomb on the evening of Good Friday.

2.) His soul descends into the realm of the dead to announce to the Just the tidings of their redemption.

3.) Fearing the body of Jesus will be taken, the chief priests place guards at the tomb.

4.) On the third day Jesus rises from the dead, glorious and immortal.

5.) The earth quakes as the angel rolls back the stone, and the guards flee in terror.

6.) The holy women coming to anoint the body of Jesus are amazed and frightened to find the tomb open.

7.) An angel calms their fears: "He is not here. He has risen as He said."

8.) Jesus appears to Mary Magdalen and Peter and two disciples on the way to Emmaus.

9.) That evening He appears to the apostles behind locked doors: "Peace be to you . . . do not be afraid."

10.) Jesus breathes on them and gives them the power to forgive sin.

2.) The Ascension of Jesus Into Heaven

1.) Jesus remains on earth forty days after His Resurrection to prove He has truly risen from the dead.

2.) He commissions the apostles to preach the gospel to every creature, and promises to be with them forever.

3.) He will not leave them orphans, but will send the Holy Spirit to enlighten and strengthen them.

4.) Jesus proceeds to Mt. Olivet accompanied by His Mother and the apostles and disciples.

5.) Extending His pierced hands over all in a last blessing, He ascends into heaven.

6.) As He ascends a cloud takes Him from their sight.

7.) Jesus ascends to take His place at the right hand of the Father.

8.) What jubilation there must be amid the angels of heaven at the triumphant entry of Jesus.

9.) The wounds in his glorified body are an endless plea before the Father on our behalf.

10.) The disciples leave Mt. Olivet and "return to Jerusalem with great joy."

3.) The Descent of the Holy Spirit

1.) The apostles are gathered in the upper room where Jesus held the Last Supper.

2.) They are persevering in prayer with Mary the Mother of Jesus.

3.) A sound comes from heaven like the rush of a mighty wind, and it fills the whole house.

4.) The Holy Spirit descends on each of them in the form of tongues of fire.

5.) Filled with the Gifts of the Holy Spirit, they are enlightened and strengthened to spread the gospel.

6.) Having lost all fear of the Jewish leaders, the apostles boldly preach Christ crucified.

7.) The multitudes are confounded because every man hears them speak in his own tongue.

8.) The Holy Spirit comes upon the infant church, never to leave it.

9.) That first day, Peter goes forth to preach and baptizes 3,000.

10.) The feast of Pentecost is the birthday of the Church, for on that day it begins to grow.

4.) The Assumption of Mary Into Heaven

1.) After the apostles have dispersed, the Blessed Mother goes to live with John, the beloved disciple.

2.) Mary lives many years on earth after the death of Christ.

3.) She is a source of comfort and consolation and strength to the apostles.

4.) As she had nourished the infant Jesus, so she nourishes spiritu-ally the infant Chuch.

5.) Mary dies, not of bodily infirmity, but is wholly ravished in a rapture of divine love.

6.) After her burial the Apostles go to the tomb and find only fragrant lilies.

7.) Jesus does not permit the sinless body of His Mother to decay in the grave.

8.) Corruption of the body is an effect of original sin, from which Mary is totally exempted.

9.) The bodies of all mankind, at the last judgment, will be brought back and united again to the soul.

10.) Mary's assumption favors Mary's full communion not only with Christ, but with each one of us. She is beside us.

5.) The Coronation of Mary

1.) As Mary enters heaven, the entire court of heaven greets with joy this masterpiece of God's creation.

2.) Mary is crowned by her divine Son as Queen of heaven and earth.

3.) More than we can ever know, the Hearts of Jesus and Mary overflow with joy at this reunion.

4.) Only in heaven will we know the great majesty of that coronation, and the joy it gave to the angels and saints.

5.) Even the angels, who by nature are greater than humans, hail Mary as their Queen.

6.) Mary shares so fully in the glory of Christ because she shared so fully in His suffering.

7.) Only in heaven will we see how central is the role of Mary in the divine plan of redemption.

8.) The angels and saints longed for the coming of her whose heel crushes the head of the serpent.

9.) Mary pleads our cause as the most powerful Queen and a most merciful and loving Mother.

10.) A great sign appeared in heaven; a woman clothed with the sun, the moon under her feet, and on her head a crown of 12 stars.

(These meditations on the Joyful, Sorrowful, and Glorious mysteries were taken, with permission, from the booklet Praying the Rosary Without Distractions, *published by The Rosary Center, PO Box 3617, Portland, Oregon 97208.)*

Pius XII is known as the "friend of sport." He viewed exercise and sports as ways of tempering the character and forming the will as hard as steel.

5

Teachings of Pope Pius XII

P ope Pius XII was born in Rome on March 2, 1876. His
pontificate lasted from March 2, 1939 to October 9, 1958.
He was an avid swimmer and was the first Pope to install
a gymnasium in the Vatican. He is known as the "friend of sport."
He viewed exercise and sports as ways of tempering the character
and forming the will as hard as steel. I remember when I was
studying physical education in college in Montana that I came
upon a book with Pius XII's teachings on exercise and sports. I
thought he must have had, with his depth of knowledge, a degree
in physical education! The following teachings on sports are in
the form of allocutions, papal teaching addresses given to groups
of people.

THE SPORTING IDEAL
(Given in Rome on May 20, 1945)

Both those who accuse the Church of not caring for the
body and physical culture, and those who want to restrict Her
competence and activity to things described as "purely religious"
and "exclusively spiritual," are far from the truth. As if the body,
a creation of God like the soul to which it is united, did not
have its part to play in the homage to be rendered to the Creator!
"In eating, in drinking," wrote the Apostle of the Gentiles to the
Corinthians, "in all that you do, do everything as for God's glory"

117

(1 Cor. 10:31). St. Paul here is speaking of physical activity. In the phrase "in all that you do," therefore, may well be understood the care of the body, "sport"! He often speaks of sport explicitly, in fact: of races, of fights, and not in a spirit of criticism or condemnation, but as one acquainted with them, and ennobling them with his Christian conception.

In the final analysis, what is sport if not a form of education for the body? This education is closely related to morality. How then could the Church not care about it?

And in fact, the Church has always shown for the body a care and respect which materialism, with its idolatrous cult, has never manifested. Which is, after all, quite natural, considering that materialism sees in the body naught but flesh, whose strength and beauty bud and flower only to fade and die, like the grasses of the field which finish as dust of the earth. The Christian concept is very different. The human body is, in its own right, God's masterpiece and the order of visible creation. The Lord has intended that it should flourish here below and enjoy immortality in the glory of heaven. He has linked it to spirit in the unity of the human nature, to give to the soul a taste of the enchantment of the works of God's hands, to help it to see the Creator of them both in his mirror, and so to know, adore, and love Him. It is not God who made the body mortal. It was sin! But if because of sin the body, made from the clay of the earth, must one day return to dust (1 Cor. 6:19-20), God will nonetheless form it again from the dust and recall it to life. Thus the Church respects even the body reduced to dust, because it will rise again.

But the Apostle Paul leads us on to a still nobler vision: "Surely you know that your bodies are the shrines of the Holy Spirit who dwells in you. And He is God's gift to you, so that you are no longer your own masters. A great price was paid to ransom you; glorify God by making your bodies the Shrines of His presence."

Glorify God by making your bodies the shrines of His presence! Shrines of the Holy Spirit! Do you not recognize there, beloved children, the very same words which recur time and again in the psalms? Praise God and glorify Him in His holy temple!

But then it must be said of the human body, too: "Domum tuam decet sanctitas, Domine" (Ps. 92:5)! Thy house must needs be holy, O Lord! We must love and cultivate the dignity, the harmony, the chaste beauty of this temple: "Domine, diligo habitaculum domus tuae, et locum tabernaculi gloriae tuae," "How well, Lord, I love Thy house in its beauty, the place where Thy own glory dwells" (Ps. 25:8).

Now what is the prime purpose and object of sport, understood in a healthy and Christian sense, if not precisely to cultivate the dignity and harmony of the human body, to develop its health, strength, agility, and grace?

And let no one reprove St. Paul his bold expression: "I buffet my own body and make it my slave" (1 Cor. 9:27). For in that same passage, Paul is basing himself on the example of the keen athletes! You are well aware from personal experience that sport, undertaken with conscious moderation, fortifies the body, gives it health, makes it fresh and strong; but to achieve this work of education, it subjects the body to a rigorous discipline which dominates it and really makes it a slave: training in stamina, resistance to pain, a severe habit of continence and temperance, are all indispensable conditions to carry off the victory. Sport is an effective antidote to softness and easy living. It awakens the sense of order and forms the man in self-examination and mastery of self, in despising danger without either boasting or cowardice. So you see already how it goes far beyond mere physical strength and leads man to moral strength and greatness. This is what Cicero with incomparable lucidity of style expressed when he wrote: "Exercendum . . corpus et ita afficiendum est, ut obeodire consilio rationiqu posit in exsequendis negotiis et in labore tolerando." "The body should be so treated and trained as to be able to obey the counsel of wisdom and reason, whether it be a matter of work to be done or trials to be borne." From the birthplace of sport came also the proverbial phrase "fair play": that knightly and courteous emulation which raises the spirit above meanness and deceit and the dark subterfuges of vanity and vindictiveness, and preserves it from the excesses of a closed and intransigent nationalism. Sport is the school of loyalty, of courage, of fortitude, of resolution and universal brotherhood: all natural virtues, these, but which form for the supernatural virtues a sound foundation, and prepare man to carry without weakness the weight of the greatest responsibilities.

How could we fail on this occasion to recall the example of our great Predecessor, Pius XI, who was also a master of the sport of mountaineering? Read again the description, so striking in its calm simplicity, of the night which he spent after a difficult 20 hours' climb, upon a sharp spur of rock on Mount Rosa, 4600 metres above sea level in an icy cold wind, standing up without being able to take a step in any direction, without being able to surrender for even a moment to sleep, in the center of that most grandiose of all the grandiose mountain scenery, before that the most imposing exhibition of the omnipotence and majesty of God. What physical power of resistance, what moral tenacity such behavior supposes! And what a fitting preparation those bold ventures were for the intrepid courage he would need in carrying out the formidable duties which would one day be his in facing seemingly insoluble problems, as Head of the Church.

To exhaust the body within healthy limits in order to rest the mind and prepare it for new work, to sharpen the senses in order to acquire greater intensity and penetration in the intellectual faculties, to exercise the muscles and become accustomed to effort in order to temper the character and form a will as hard and elastic as steel . . . that was the idea which the mountaineer priest had of sport.

How distant this idea is from vulgar materialism, for which the body is all there is of man. And how distant it is, too, from that prideful madness which cannot resist ruining the health and strength of the athlete in unhealthy exaggeration simply in order to carry off the honors in some boxing bout or competition at high speeds and which at times does not hesitate to expose his life to danger. Sport which is worthy of the name makes man courageous in the face of danger, but does not authorize his undergoing a grave risk without proportionate cause. This would be morally illicit. Pius XI wrote on this point: "When I say 'true danger' I mean a state of affairs which either by its very nature, or due to the dispositions of the person subject to it, cannot presumably be faced without some evil resulting." Hence he commented on his climb of Mount Rosa: "We did not have the least intention of attempting what is called a 'desperate gamble'! True mountaineering is not a sport for breaknecks, but is all a question of prudence, and a little courage, strength, fortitude, and love for nature and her most hidden treasures."

Thus conceived, sport is not an end in itself, but a means. As such, it is and must remain subordinated to its end, which consists in the perfect and balanced formation and education of the whole man, for whom sport is an aid in the ready and joyful accomplishment of his duties: be they in his sphere of work, be they in the family.

With a lamentable reversal of the natural scale of values, some young people passionately dedicate their whole interest and activity to sports meetings and events, to training for matches, with their ideal in life being a championship . . . while they give only half-hearted attention to the demanding needs of their study and profession! The home becomes for them only a hotel, where like strangers they occasionally put up when passing!

Thank God that you are different, dear children! For after a fine game you return to your work with a renewed strength and vigor, and in the home you raise the spirits of the whole family with your enthusiastic description of your experiences.

Sport, which is at the service of a healthy, strong, full life, of a more fruitful activity in the fulfillment of the duties of state, can and should be also at the service of God. In fact, it encourages one in this direction by the physical strength and the moral virtues which it develops; but while the pagan subjected himself to the strict regime of sport to obtain a merely corruptible crown, the Christian subjects himself to the same with a nobler aim, for an immortal reward.

Have you ever noticed the considerable number of soldiers among the martyrs whom the Church venerates? Their body and character formed by the training inherent to the profession of arms, they were at least the equal of their comrades in their country's service, in strength, in courage; but they proved themselves to be incomparably superior to them by their readiness to fight and sacrifice themselves in the loyal service of Christ and of his Church. Animated by the same faith and by the same spirit, may you, too, be disposed to put everything in second place after your duties as Christians.

What would be the use of physical courage and boldness of character be if the Christian employed them only for earthly ends, to win some cup, or to give himself the airs of a superman? If he were unable, when necessary, to rob a half-hour of sleep or put off an appointment at the sports ground in order to attend Sunday Mass? If he could not conquer human respect in order to practice and defend his religion? If he did not use his superiority or authority to prevent or halt with a look, a word, or a gesture, some blasphemy, evil speech, dishonesty, or to protect the younger and weaker members from provocation and suspect companionship? If he could not make a habit of concluding his sporting successes with a praise of God, Creator and Lord of nature, and all of his own faculties?

Be conscious of the fact that the greatest honor and the most holy destiny of the body is its being the dwelling of a soul which radiates moral purity and is sanctified by divine grace.

Thus, beloved sons, we have outlined the purpose of sport. Strive earnestly now to put this into practice, conscious that in the field of physical culture the Christian concept needs to receive nothing from outside, but has much to give. No less than others, you, too, can accept and adopt that which in the various sporting meetings is truly good. But in what concerns the place which sport should have in human life, for the individual, for the family and the community, the Catholic ideal is a safeguard and an enlightenment. The experience of the past decades has been most instructive in this sense: it has proved that only the Christian attitude toward sport can effectively combat false concepts and pernicious tendencies, and prevent their evil influence. In compensation, it enriches physical culture with all which tends to raise the spiritual value of man. What is more, it directs sport towards a noble exultation of the dignity, vigor, and efficiency of life fully and strongly Christian. When he remains faithful to the tenets of his faith, the apostolate of the sportsman consists in this.

It is noticeable how very often the Apostle Paul uses sporting images to illustrate his apostolic life and the life of struggle of the Christian on earth. This stands out particularly in the first Letter to the Corinthians: "You know well enough," he writes," that when men run in a race, the race is for all, but the prize for one; run, then, for victory" (1 Cor. 9:24). And he goes on in a passage to which we have already referred: "Every athlete must keep all his appetites under control; and he does it to win a crown that fades, whereas ours is imperishable. So I do not run my course like a man in doubt of his goal; I do not fight my battle like a man who wastes his blows on the air. I buffet my own body, and make it my slave; or I, who have preached to others, may myself be rejected as worthless" (1 Cor. 9:25-27).

These words illumine the concept of sport with a mystical radiance. But what matters to the Apostle is the superior reality of which sport is the image and symbol: unceasing work for Christ, the restraining and subjection of the body to the immortal soul, eternal life - the prize of this struggle. For the Christian athlete and for you too, beloved sons, sport must not be the supreme ideal, the ultimate goal, but must serve and tend towards that goal. If a sporting activity is for you a recreation and stimulus which aids you in better fulfilling your duties of work and study, then it can be said that it is being used in its true sense and is attaining its true end.

If, as well, sport is for you not only an image, but also in some way the execution of your noblest duty, if, that is to say, in your sporting activity you render your body more docile and obedient to the soul and to your moral obligations, if, furthermore, by your example you contribute to modern sporting activity a form which better corresponds to the dignity of man and the commandments of God, then you are in one and the same activity putting into effect the symbol and the thing symbolized, as St. Paul explained it. And then one day you will be able to say with the great Apostle: "I have fought the good fight; I have finished the race; I have redeemed my pledge; I look forward to the prize that is waiting for me, the prize I have earned. The Lord, the judge whose award never goes amiss, will grant it to me when that day comes; to me, yes, and to all those who learned to welcome His coming" (2 Tim. 4:7-8).

(Conclusion)

SPORT AT THE SERVICE OF THE SPIRIT
(Given in Rome on July 29, 1945)

In bidding you a cordial welcome today, we are conscious that this is an exceptional group. As directors and instructors of the Central Sports School, you represent the effort to develop man's physical powers and train his character; as graduates of many American universities, you represent the striving of man for those higher values which are recalled by the very name of the university; and finally, as a unit under military direction, you suggest the discipline by which the spiritual and the physical, the body and the soul, must be brought into harmony, the harmony of the complete man.

Sport, properly directed, develops character, makes a man courageous, a generous loser, and a gracious victor; it refines the senses, gives us intellectual penetration, steels the will to endurance. It is not merely a physical development, then. Sport, rightly understood, is an occupation of the whole man, and while perfecting the body as an instrument of the mind, it also makes the mind itself a more refined instrument of the search and communication of truth and helps man to achieve that end to which all others must be subservient, the service and praise of his Creator.

It is for this reason that we must rejoice to see the direction of the Central Sports School in the hands of university men. For you will insist on the one hand on the immense help sport can give towards a man's perfecting his faculties for the struggle of life; while your academic associations will put you on your guard against the tendency, too common, alas, nowadays, of making sport an end in itself - which it never can be.

The harmony between the physical development of man on the one side and his intellectual and moral education on the other is not easy to achieve. Hence the necessity of your instilling into your pupils the importance of discipline - not a merely external discipline, but the discipline of rigorous self-control, which is as momentous in the realm of sport as it is in that of the intellectual or moral order.

CYCLING
(Given on June 26, 1946)

We would now like to point out why the sport of racing merits special consideration, both for what it is in itself and for its value as a symbol.

A race demands and supposes an effort, a healthy effort, a combined effort of the whole body, an effort whose power is manifested not so much by violent spurts and impulses, as in the courageous, manly, disciplined and continuous output of energy, sustained till the finish line is reached.

But above all, how noble and resplendent is the reality of which this sport is a symbol! In the race towards eternal life and glory, you battle not to win a corruptible crown which may pass into the hands of others, but with the hope of an incorruptible crown. It is a race in which none of you run the risk of being disappointed at not gaining victory, provided that you are loyal to the rules of this sublime competition of the spirit and do not allow either tiredness or any obstacle to halt you until the goal is reached.

Go, therefore, under the radiant sunshine of Italy, of this your fatherland whose natural beauties you know and whose worthy and valorous champions you wish to be. Go, bold contestants both in the earthly race and the eternal.

LESSONS OF THE MOUNTAIN
(Given on September 25, 1948)

A sentiment of devout homage has inspired you with the desire of receiving Our Blessing and encouragement on the occasion of your sixtieth National Congress. What advice could we give better suited to your character as Alpinists than this simple recommendation: learn the lessons of the mountain? It is a lesson of spiritual uplifting, a lesson more of moral than physical strength. Our intrepid Predecessor Pius XI, in recalling his past experiences as a mountaineer, used to describe them under a double aspect: the irresistible attraction of heights, and the healthy, exultant attraction of the difficulties to be overcome.

The common man likes to have his feet firmly planted on solid earth. You aspire instead to go climbing ever high; on the power of your muscles, it is true . . . yet this yearning for altitude is in the depths of the heart the echo of a need of mind, heart, and soul. Why climb higher and higher? Why want to?

First of all, in order to see further, to look out from a better vantage point. You do not want to be like those who "cannot see the wood for the trees." As you climb up and up, the view extends further and further, the scene appears in all its splendid grandeur, the particulars melt into the whole picture and take on their right perspective. The intersecting outlines of hills and valleys, streams and rivers, combine into a harmonious unity. In the same way, too, the apparent incoherencies of life take on an harmonious unity when the action of Divine Providence is seen with a wider vision, from a higher vantage point.

Excelsior; still higher!

When the sky is clear, it lights up the earth at your feet. If the mist clothes the plain and wraps it in a mantle of darkness, you instead are up in the light, and the sea of clouds gleams snow-white below you, gilded by the light from above. In like manner, when one looks towards God, up to heaven, the sufferings and worries of this earth cannot hide the blue of changeless Christian hope, and the very uncertainties and troubles are transfigured by the rays of the eternal sun.

Still higher!

The confused, discordant noises of useless argument, or the futile nonsense of earth, the conflicts of self-love and mean interests, die out on the mountain, are lost in the majestic silence which is no whit disturbed by the soft murmurs or solemn rumbles of nature. And when the echo of thunder, or falls, or landslides rebounds from peak to peak, the heart, filled with emotion or anxiety, feels nonetheless more at ease in the midst of the purposeless and wicked chit-chat of man. Blessed is he who can dominate the worldly bustle which surrounds him, and savor in silence and recollection the peace of God.

Higher still in the cool, rare atmosphere of the mountain, the air penetrates into the remotest nooks of the lung tissue, and purges them of remnants of stale air. The heart beats more strongly and produces a more vigorous circulation, bringing a more intense life to the whole organism. And so, too, in the calm of the spirit, in the serene breathing of prayer, the soul is elevated, purified, vivified, more free, and more strong.

There comes a time, however, when the mountain seems to turn hostile. It appears then to want to protect itself or have its revenge on those who would violate its virginal solitude. It offers them nothing now. It casts them off. Sometimes it strikes them down mercilessly.

Everybody knows of the dramatic assault many times repeated by bold climbers, against the formidable Mount Everest in the Himalayas. Neither the great sufferings, nor incessant danger, nor exhaustion, nor the remembrance of those who had died, could weaken the will to begin anew.

While it is true that they hope to serve science and humanity by wresting from the altitudes their secrets, it must be admitted too that there is another force which drives them on. They are driven by a powerful interior impulse, by a mysterious passion for struggle at any cost, against difficulty, to overcome obstacles.

This tendency, when it is not shackled but guided by reason (and not by thoughtless temerity) is an aspect of the virtue of fortitude whose role it is, according to the Angelic Doctor, to make reason prevail over exhaustion caused by physical pain: "Dacit virtus fortitudinis, ut ratio non absorbeatur a corporalibus doloribus" (*Summa Theologica*, 2a2ae, q. 123, a.8).

- - -

John Paul II loved physical exercise.
When he became Pope, he exercised first thing
at 5 a.m. From the beginning, he was known as
the "athlete Pope."

6

John Paul II:
The Athlete Pope

Karol Wojtyla (John Paul II) was born in 1920 in Wadowice, Poland, a small town in the Beskidy Mountains and not far from Krakow. He was affectionately called Lolek by his parents and friends. His mother, Emilia, died of heart and kidney failure in 1929 when Lolek was nine years old. Lolek's father brought his two sons to the Marian shrine of Kalwaria in the mountains, six miles from Wadowice on the way to Krakow, to meditate and reflect after the death of their mother. He hoped that this would help his sons to hope and understand, and to help his words transmit the truth he had difficulty communicating.

After his mother's death, Lolek and his father, Lieutenant Karol Wojtyla, Sr., were left alone in their second floor apartment on Churchill Street. During World War I, Lolek's father's heroic actions had been publicly rewarded with the Iron Cross of Merit. The army sent him into retirement in 1927 with a promotion to captain because of meritorious conduct. People in Wadowice respectfully called him "the Captain." Lolek's older brother, Edmund, attended medical school in Krakow. Edmund and his father helped Lolek regain confidence in himself and in life after he lost his dear mother. This helped him to overcome the depression he experienced at this time.

Lolek's father instilled in him the discipline of and passion for physical activity. They would joyfully play soccer in the living

Lolek is seen here with his mother, Emilia, and his father, Karol, Sr. (above). Karol, Sr. brought his two sons to the Marian shrine of Kalwaria (below) after the death of Lolek's mother. The Pope would come here often during his life and would be seen contemplating and praying the Rosary.

After his mother's death, Lolek and his father were left
alone in the second floor apartment (above) next to the
parish church. They would joyfully play socer in the liv-
ing room with a ball made of rags. Karol graduated from
Wadowita State Secondary School in 1938 (below).

room with a ball made of rags. They would also read the Bible and pray the Rosary together. Lolek's father was an admirable and exceptional man, and was the mentor of spiritual life for Lolek, especially in the area of prayer. Lolek would often wake to find his father on his knees, just as he would see him in church. Lolek's brother Edmund, who was nicknamed Mundek, was Lolek's hero. He was very athletic looking, with blond hair, blue eyes, and full of energy. A friend described him as "robust and masculine." Mundek was a great athlete who loved tennis and soccer. He was 14 years older than Lolek, and inspired in his younger sibling a great love for physical activity and sports. Lolek wanted to be like his brother. When he came home from medical school in Krakow, he would take Lolek hiking, skiing, and to soccer games. Mundek died in 1932 of scarlet fever, two years out of medical school. He died in a hospital in Bielsko. The Pope was always attached to the memory of his brother and always kept his brother's stethoscope in a drawer of his desk as a wonderful treasure.

As a young boy, Lolek loved playing soccer. He played goalie and was named "Martyna" by his friends, after a well-known soccer player. He also ran track. In high school, he participated in the hundred meter run and the long jump at the Blonie, a big field by the river in Krakow. He also enjoyed palant, a game in which a stick was bounced into the air and hit by another stick. He also played table tennis with his Jewish friend, Jurek Kluger. It is known that Lolek excelled at these games. He also enjoyed dancing and was very good at it. The Polish have a phrase for Karol Wojtyla: "a man for dancing and the Rosary."

His gym teacher in high school, Czeslaw Panzakiewicz, helped him discover the excitement and challenge of hiking and coming into contact with nature. Lolek graduated from Marcin Wadowita State Secondary School in 1938. Needless to say, he received a very good grade in physical education class. He attended a public school rather than a Catholic school, and the soccer team at his school consisted mostly of Jewish boys. His contact with Jewish boys in school helped him to better understand the Jewish people. John Paul II always had an openhearted and warm

Behind his high school was the soccer field (above) where he played. Karol loved playing soccer. He played goalie. Karol, closest to the ball, is seen playing soccer (below) in 1959 in Jeziorakiem. He was a bishop at the time.

Photo courtesy of Stanislow Rybicki

relationship with the Jewish community.

Lolek liked to swim in the summer in the Skawa River. He liked to ski in the Tatra Mountains and play hockey in the winter. The Tatras are the highest mountains in Poland and the only ones of the Alpine type which reach an altitude of a little over 7,500 ft. The whole Tatra mountain area has been declared a national park. Lolek loved riding a bicycle, for both exercise and as a means of transportation. As he grew older, bike riding was one of his favorite relaxations. On his bike he often took off into the high Tatras and enjoyed God's beautiful creation. He would often go on extended bike rides with his students, as well.

It is written that when John Paul II was young, his prayer with Our Lord in St. Mary's Church in Wadowice would often come after his physical exercise and sports, such as a soccer match, a ski excursion, or just kicking the ball. Karol Wojtyla had always combined outdoor activity and exercise with spiritual development: prayer and meditation.

Skiing was the sport Lolek loved best. When he was 10 years old, he started to ski on a hill named Czuma, not far from his house in Wadowice. There was something about the purity of snow that appealed to him. He described skiing down the mountain slopes as an "extraordinary sensation." A friend called him "one of the daredevil skiers of the Tatras," adding, "He loved the thrill of it." He tried to go on a skiing vacation at least once a year, and loved Zakopane, a sort of capital of winter sports in Poland. It is located at the foot of the Tatras in southern Poland. The Tatra and Beskidy mountains were Lolek's favorite places for rest and relaxation. John Paul II had been called "theologian of the mountains" and "Pope of the mountain people," as mountain hiking and skiing developed in him the robust courage needed to overcome all kinds of obstacles. Hiking and skiing in the mountains developed in him, like Pope Pius XI, an iron will.

When he skied, Lolek would sometimes be towed up the hill by horses, and at other times he would carry his skis on his shoulders and walk to the very top of the mountain, meditating on the passion and suffering of Christ. Lolek never bothered about fancy skiing attire, but preferred baggy pants and old-fashioned

Lolek (above) loved riding a bicycle for both relaxation and as a means of transportation. He rode his bike in the Wolski Forest (below) on the outskirts of Krakow.

Lolek's bike is seen here in the papal museum in Krakow (above), along with skis and athletic jerseys given to him when he was Pope. On his bike he often took off into the Tatra Mountains and enjoyed God's creation.

Lolek liked to swim in the Skawa River (above) in the summer. In high school, he ran track. He participated in the 100-meter race and the long jump at the Blonie (below), a large field in Krakow.

Karol Wojtyla enjoyed kayaking in the summer. He enjoyed it so much that in 1955, he entered an international kayaking competition.

boots. He also preferred old-fashioned skis made of Polish hickory instead of new fiberglass ones made in the United States that were gifts from friends. When he was made Bishop, he kidded a fellow Bishop, an ardent golfer, about how foolish it was to follow a white ball around when instead he could learn how to ski.

As a young parish priest, Lolek played soccer and volleyball with the young people and organized volleyball and soccer tournaments. He also enjoyed kayaking in the summer. In 1954, he spent several days kayaking, discovering how enjoyable an activity it is. He enjoyed it so much that in 1955, he entered an international kayaking competition. Karol Wojtyla would come to be known as a great mountain hiker. In 1954, he won an award from the Polish Tourist Society for the number of miles he had hiked. He preferred going up mountains rather than down them. He would come to give mountain hiking the description of an activity that "develops character," as it developed in him an iron constitution. He would always find time to hike through the hills and forest near Krakow.

Karol Wojtyla would often take Polish youth on hiking, canoeing, and ski trips. The young nicknamed him the "eternal teenager" and also called him Wujek, or uncle. Every mountain hike began with Mass celebrated on a makeshift altar made of either a backpack or trunk of a tree. He would use these hikes to discuss various subjects, covering all aspects of life. When hiking in the mountains with his university students, he was known for saying: "What emotion one feels looking at the world from above and contemplating this magnificent panorama from all angles. The eye does not tire of admiring, nor the heart of ascending ever further."[46] After Karol Wojtyla was made Pope, the idea was born of creating a network in the mountains of Poland called "Paths of the Pope" - that is, the hiking paths which were used by him years ago. A guidebook has been published in Poland with information about the routes taken and visited on the Pope's hikes years ago.

In 1960, two years after Karol Wojtyla became a Bishop at age 38, Dr. Stanislaw Kownocki prescribed lots of exercise for him, lots of intense activity and plenty of movement. The doctor prescribed it specifically for Karol's anemia. When Karol Wojtyla

Karol Wojtyla loved skiing. It was his favorite sport. He would go to Zakopane, located at the foot of the Tatra Mountains, and ski (above). He would hike on paths on Mt. Tatra (below), as the author is seen on a bike on one of them in June of 2005.

was a Cardinal, he would exercise first thing every morning for one-half hour, from 5 to 5:30 a.m. before prayer and meditation. He was in such great shape at the age of 58 that a friend, Fr. Malinski, reported that he could swim back and forth one mile across a lake without even pausing for a rest. Cardinal Wojtyla once visited Michigan to give a three-day conference. He refused to give talks one of the three days because he needed to get away and get some exercise.

When he became Pope, John Paul II exercised first thing, at 5 a.m. on the roof terrace built by Paul VI. From the beginning, he was known as the "athlete Pope." One of the priests on the Vatican staff became concerned and thought the Pope would have the entire staff doing physical exercises. John Paul II loved physical activity as a form of relaxation and was often seen walking in his private gardens or playing tennis. He had the Vatican tennis court made fit for use, as Paul VI, not known for being athletic, had turned it into a helicopter pad. He had a natural need to exercise. Along with brisk walks in his garden, John Paul II would swim in the summer and work off extra energy. He had a 25-meter swimming pool especially built at his summer house at Castel Gandolfo, 20 miles east of Rome.

Early in his papacy, John Paul II continued his passion for skiing and hiking in the mountains. He encouraged those who climb mountains to be comtemplatives, to contemplate the beauty of the mountains and the grandeur of the peaks, and to let the spirit lift them up to God in prayer. The Pope went to the Trentino and Valle d'Aosta Alps in northern Italy for many summer vacations, where he would climb the mountains. On September 8, 1986, John Paul II was taken by helicopter to Mt. Blanc, a mountain loved by Pier Giorgio Frassati. When he took the first steps on the untouched snow and immersed himself in the beautiful surroundings, he spoke of the quiet in the mountains, a quiet in which man can hear more clearly the interior echo of the voice of God.

When visiting the mountains, John Paul II always spoke of Mary, his dear heavenly mother. In the heart of the Dolomite Mountains in northern Italy, on August 26, 1979, he said:

Early in his papacy, John Paul II hiked and skied in the Alps in northern Italy. On September 8, 1986, he was taken by helicopter to Mt. Blanc (above), a mountain loved by Pier Giorgio Frassati. John Paul II is seen shooting a basketball (below) at a playground with children. Oh, how the young loved him!

"Modern man must lift his gaze and raise it high. He feels more and more the danger of an exclusive attachment to the earth. How much easier it is to lift our eyes upward when they meet those of that sweet Mother who is entirely simplicity and love."[47]

When he took vacations in the mountains early in his papacy, the Pope often disregarded his planned itinerary in order to continue climbing. On July 20, 1989 in Les Combes, in northern Italy, he said: "The mountains are a challenge; they provoke man, the human person, the young and not only the young, to make an effort to surpass himself."[48] The Pope climbed mountains with great perseverance, continuing to walk for hours until he reached the top. While the Pope was still able to climb mountains, he never stopped halfway. He would walk with the help of a wooden walking stick and lean on it when the path became steep. When leaning on it, he would pray, meditate, and enjoy the sun, air, wind, and mountain streams. When vacationing in the mountains, John Paul II loved to hear traditional mountain folk songs and loved to mix with people he met along the way who lived in the mountains. Surely at these times, this would bring back memories for this "athlete Pope" of the people living in the mountains back in Zakopane and the high Tatra mountains in his beloved Poland.

Over the weekend of the Jubilee of Sports, October 28-29 during the Jubilee year 2000, thousands of athletes crossed the threshold of the Holy Door of St. Peter's Basilica as a sign of conversion. In a Saturday morning meeting with 5,000 athletes and sports enthusiasts, John Paul II addressed them in the Vatican auditorium. The theme of the meeting was "The Face and Soul of Sport at the Time of the Jubilee." In his address, the Pope spoke of the authentic face of sport, at a time when it risked being hurt by commercialization and thus the real value of it stifled. John Paul II spoke to the athletes of sports as a "language all understand." He spoke of sports not only expressing man's physical abilities, but also his intellectual and spiritual capacity.

John Paul II told those in attendance that they must not be carried away by the obsession of physical perfection, as sport is not only physical power and muscular efficiency, but also soul. He

On October 29, 2000, John Paul II celebrated Mass in Rome's Olympic Stadium before 70,000 athletes. Two young athletes bring up the offertory gifts (above). John Paul II is seen talking with a handicapped athlete (below) at the 2000 Jubilee of Sports in Rome.

also warned the athletes that they must not allow themselves to be subjugated by the harsh laws of production and consumption. Too, he spoke to them of not being carried away by utilitarian and hedonistic considerations. He spoke of the importance of reverencing the dignity of the body and not betraying it. He also spoke of the noble ideas of sport. The Holy Father spoke of values that sports can promote, such as fraternity, magnanimity, honesty, and respect for the body - values that are indispensable for any good athlete. He also warned that sport can seek only profit, and instead of uniting, it can divide.

The Pope stressed that the key is to promote sports as a means of enhancing the dignity of the human person and respecting the needs of the human person. John Paul II always gave us a vision of sports based on the principle that the dignity of the human person is the goal and criterion of all sporting activity. The Holy Father concluded this meeting by reminding the athletes that "rhythms of society" and some sports competitions might make the Christian forget the need to worship God in the liturgical assembly on Sunday, the Day of the Lord and the day of a merited and just rest. He, like Pius XII before him, stressed the importance of not letting anything interfere with the faithful's obligation in this regard.

On October 29, 2000 John Paul II celebrated Mass in Rome's Olympic Stadium before 70,000 athletes, which was followed by a soccer game presided over by the Pope. The game was played between the Italian national team and a team of foreign players. Before the Mass, Antonio Rossi, gold medallist in canoeing in Atlanta and Sydney 2000, became the spokesman for all athletes. Rossi quoted St. Catherine of Siena: "If you are what you are meant to be, you will set the world on fire." He stated that this motto must be the dream and objective for all athletes in the new millennium. Juan Antonio Samaranch, president of the International Olympic Committee, also spoke and gave thanks to John Paul II for the support he has given to sports over the years.

During his homily at the Mass, John Paul II talked about sports having become one of the typical phenomena of modernity and a kind of "sign of the times." He also urged a call to conversion on the part of athletes, which requires an "examination of conscience." He called for all to analyze situations of transgression into which sport can fall and for athletes, especially professionals, to pronounce their "mea culpa." The Pope spoke to athletes the day before in a special meeting. He spoke of sports not being free of temptations, and he warned that signs of unrest are evident, and that the ethical values of sport are being challenged.

Athletes in collaboration with the Holy See had written a "Sports Manifesto" to help guide players in the new millennium, and the Pope discussed this manifesto in his homily. The manifesto refers to competition having ethical, spiritual, and religious dimensions, along with functioning in recreational, cultural, educational, and social ways. It also refers to competition as contributing to the development of human capacities, helping to appreciate life, the great gift of God. The manifesto clearly condemns all that unethically alters performance or endangers an athlete's health. The manifesto also states that sports can't be a source of division between weak and strong, rich or poor. That winning and profits cannot deprive sports of its moral value and violate the rights of children and youth.

On May 30, 2004, John Paul II encouraged sports to be promoted as a way to free young people from the snares of apathy and indifference, and to arouse a healthy sense of competition in them. He showed sports to contribute to the love of life, teaching sacrifice, respect, responsibility, and leading to the full development of every human person. He stated:

> St. Paul the Apostle proposed the image of the athlete to the Christians of Corinth in order to illustrate Christian life and as an example of effort and constancy (1 Cor. 9:24-25). Indeed, the correct practice of sport must be accompanied by moderation and training in self-discipline. The Christian can find sports helpful for developing the cardinal virtues of prudence, justice, fortitude, and temperance in the race for the wreath that is "imperishable," as St. Paul writes.[49]

On June 26, 2004 the Pope encouraged a sporting mindset

and culture that will promote "doing sport" and not only "talking about sport" that will help people rediscover the full truth about the human person. John Paul II stated: "In our time, organized sport sometimes seems conditioned by the logic of profit, of the spectacular, of doping, exasperated rivalry, and episodes of violence."[50] On this day, the Pope discussed the importance of proclaiming and witnessing to the humanizing power of the Gospel with regard to the practice of sport. He proposed that sports be lived out in accordance with the Christian outlook, thus becoming a generative principle of profound human relations and encouraging the building of a more serene and supportive world. On January 17, 2005, the Pope stressed how important sport is in contemporary society. The Church considers sports played with full respect for the rules an effective means of education, especially for the young generation.

John Paul II gave many allocutions, teachings on sport and exercise, to many different groups of people. The following teachings of his will shed light on the world of sport and those who participate in sports.

LET THE PRACTICE OF SPORTS ALWAYS PROMOTE PEACE
(Given in Rome on October 11, 1981)

Dear young athletes!

1.) I am happy to welcome you and cordially greet you, along with the Leaders of the Italian National Olympic Committee who have accompanied you, at the end of the national "Youth Games" competitions, to give you the opportunity to express here, also on behalf of your colleagues belonging to all the regions of Italy, the sentiments of your Christian faith and your youthful joy. I address my warm thanks to Dr. Franco Carraro, your hard-working President, for the kind words with which he has introduced this informal meeting.

2.) Your presence gives me joy not only because of the spectacle of stupendous youth that you offer to my gaze, but also because of the physical and moral values you represent. Sport, in fact, even under the aspect of physical education, finds in the Church support for all its good and wholesome elements. For the Church cannot but encourage everything that serves the harmonious development of the human body, rightly considered the masterpiece of the whole of creation, not only because of its proportion, vigour, and beauty, but also and especially because God has made it his dwelling and the instrument of an immortal soul, breathing into it that "breath of life" (cf. Gen. 2:7) by which man is made in his image and likeness. If we then consider the supernatural aspect, St. Paul's words are an illuminating admonition: "Do you not know that your bodies are members of Christ? . . .So glorify God in your body" (1 Cor 6:15; 19-20).

3.) These are, beloved young people, some features of what Revelation teaches us about the greatness and dignity of the human body, created by God and redeemed by Christ. For this reason, the Church does not cease to recommend the best use of this marvelous instrument by a suitable physical education which, while it avoids on the one hand the deviations of body worship, on the other hand it trains both body and spirit for effort, courage, balance, sacrifice, nobility, brotherhood, courtesy, and, in a word, fair play. If practiced in this way, sport will help you above all to become citizens who love social order and peace; it will teach you to see in sports competitions not struggles between rivals, not factors of division, but peaceful sporting events in which sense of respect for the competitor must never be lacking, even in the rightful effort to achieve victory.

With these thoughts and with these wishes, I very willingly impart to you, to members of your families, and to your friends, my special Apostolic Blessing, as a token of abundant heavenly graces and as a sign of my favour.

THE MOST AUTHENTIC DIMENSION OF SPORT: TO CREATE A NEW "CIVILIZATION OF LOVE" (Given in homily at Olympic Stadium in Rome on April 12, 1984)

1.) This extraordinary Holy Year would not have been complete without the witness of faith shown also by those involved in the world of sport, that human and social phenomenon which has such importance and influence on people's way of acting and thinking today. So it is a great joy for me to be with you, men and women devoted to sport, in order to celebrate the Jubilee of the Redemption accomplished by Christ through his Passion, Death, and Resurrection.

St. Paul, who had been acquainted with the sporting world of his day, in the first *Letter to the Corinthians*, which we have just listened to, writes to those Christians living in the Greek world: "Do you not know that in a race all the runners compete, but only one receives the prize? So run that you may obtain it!" (1 Cor 9:24).

Here we see that the Apostle of the Gentiles, in order

to bring the message of Christ to all peoples, drew from the concepts, images, terminologies, modes of expression, and philosophical and literary references not only of the Jewish tradition but also of Hellenic culture. And he did not hesitate to include sport among the human values which he used as points of support and reference for dialogue with the people of his time. Thus he recognized the fundamental *validity of sport*, considering it not just as a term of comparison to illustrate a higher ethical and aesthetic ideal, but also in its intrinsic reality as a factor in the *formation of man* and as a part of his culture and his civilization.

In this way St. Paul, continuing the teaching of Jesus, established the Christian attitude towards this as towards the other expressions of man's natural faculties such as science, learning, work, art, love, and social and political commitment. Not an attitude of rejection or flight, but one of respect, esteem, even though correcting and elevating them: in a word, an attitude of *redemption*.

Positive values

2.) And it is precisely this idea of Christianity accepting, adopting, perfecting, and elevating human values - and thus as a hymn to life - which I would like to pass on today to you and to all those who in whatever way and in every country of the world practice or are interested in this human activity called sport.

The Jubilee sheds the light of the Redemption also on this human and social phenomenon, exalting and emphasizing its positive values.

We cannot ignore the fact that in this field too, unfortunately, there are certain negative or at least questionable aspects which today are rightly analyzed and criticized by experts in the study of customs and behavior, aspects which undoubtedly cause suffering to yourselves.

But we also know what great efforts have been made to ensure that the "philosophy of sport" always prevails, the key principle of which is not "sport for sport's sake" or other motives than the *dignity, freedom*, and *integral development of man*!

You yourselves, in the *Sportsmen's Manifesto* that you

have launched for this Jubilee, solemnly state that "sport is at the service of man and not man at the service of sport, and therefore the dignity of the human person is the goal and criterion of all sporting activity. . .Sport is sincere and generous confrontation, a meeting place, a bond of solidarity and friendship. . .Sport can be genuine culture when the setting in which it is practiced and the experience it brings are open and sensitive to human and universal values for the balanced development of man in all his dimensions." And you also say that sport, "by reason of its universal nature, has a place on the international level as a means of brotherhood and peace," and that you wish to commit yourselves to ensuring that it "is for individuals and for the world an effective instrument of reconciliation and peace!"

Sincere fraternity

3.) Yes, dear athletes, may this truly extraordinary meeting revive within you the awareness of the need to commit yourselves so that sport contributes to making mutual love, sincere fraternity, and authentic solidarity penetrate society. For sport can make a valid and fruitful contribution to the peaceful co-existence of all peoples, above and beyond every discrimination of race, language, and nations.

According to the *Olympic Charter*, which sees sport as the occasion of "a better mutual understanding and friendship for the building of a better and more peaceful world," let your meetings be a symbolic sign for the whole of society and a prelude to that new age in which nations "shall not lift up sword against nation" (Is 2:4). Society looks to you with confidence and is grateful to you for your witness to the ideals of peaceful civil and social living together for the building up of a new civilization founded on love, solidarity, and peace.

These ideals do honor to the men and women of sport who have worked them out and proclaimed them, but in a special way they do honor to the numerous champions - some of whom are here today - who in their careers have lived and achieved these ideals with exemplary commitment!

Temple of the Spirit

4.) In the passage that we have listened to, St. Paul also emphasized the interior and spiritual significance of sport: "Every athlete exercises self-control in all things" (1 Cor. 9:25). This recognizes the healthy dose of balance, self-discipline, sobriety, and therefore, in a word, of *virtue*, which is implied in the practice of sport.

To be a good sportsman, one must have honesty with oneself and with others, loyalty, moral strength (over and above physical strength), perseverance, a spirit of collaboration and sociability, generosity, broadness of outlook and attitude, and ability to live in harmony with others and to share: all these requirements belong to the *moral order*: but St. Paul adds straight afterwards, "They (namely the athletes in the Greek and Roman stadiums) do it to receive a perishable wreath (that is, an earthly, passing, fleeting glory and reward, even when it evokes the delirium of the crowd), but we an imperishable" (1 Cor 9:25).

In these words, we find the elements for outlining not only an *anthropology* but an ethic and also a theology of sport which highlights all its value.

In the first place, sport is *making good use of the body*, an effort to reaching optimum physical condition, which brings marked consequences of psychological well-being. From our Christian faith we know that, through baptism, the human person, in his or her totality and integrity of soul and body, becomes a temple of the Holy Spirit: "Do you not know that your body is a temple of the Holy Spirit within you, which you have from God? You are not your own; you were bought with a price (that is, with the blood of Christ the Redeemer). So glorify God in your body" (1 Cor 6:19-20).

Sport is *competitiveness*, a contest for winning a crown, a cup, a title, a first place. But from the Christian faith, we know that the "imperishable crown," the "eternal life" which is received from God as a gift but which is also the goal of a daily victory in the practice of virtue is much more valuable. And if there is a really important form of striving, again according to St. Paul it is this: "But earnestly desire the higher gifts" (1 Cor 12:31), which means the gifts that best serve the growth of the Kingdom of God in yourselves and in the world!

Sport is the *joy of life, a game, a celebration*, and as such it must be properly used and perhaps, today, freed from excess technical perfection and professionalism, through a recovery of its free nature, its ability to strengthen bonds of friendship, to foster dialogue and openness to others, as an expression of the *richness of being*, much more valid and to be prized than *having*, and hence far above the harsh laws of production and consumption and all other purely utilitarian and hedonistic considerations in life.

Gospel of love

5.) All of this, dear friends, reaches its fullness in the *Gospel of love*, which we have heard proclaimed through the words of Jesus, quoted by St. John, and which is summed up in the single commandment: *Love!*

Jesus insists: "Abide in my love. If you keep my commandments, you will abide in my love. . .

"These things I have spoken to you, and that your joy may be full. . .

"This is my commandment: that you love one another as I have loved you. . . You are my friends if you do what I command you. . .

"You did not choose me, but I chose you and appointed you that you should go and bear fruit and that your fruit should abide.

"This I command you, to love one another" (Jn 15:9-17).

On an occasion as unique and significant as this meeting of ours today, I wish to pass on to all of you, and especially to the youngsters, this message, this appeal, this commandment of Christ: Love! Love one another! Abide in the love of Christ and open up your hearts to one another! This is the secret of life, and also the deepest and most authentic dimension of sport!

To all of you I wish to say further: In this age which is

so marvelous and so tormented, strive to build a culture of love, a civilization of love! You can contribute to this by sport and by your whole behavior, by all the freshness of your feelings, and by all the seriousness of the discipline which sport can teach you. Live as people who stay friends and brothers and sisters even when you compete for the "crown" of an earthly victor! Shake hands, join your hearts in the solidarity of love and limitless cooperation! Recognize in yourselves, in each other, the sign of the Fatherhood of God and the fraternity in Christ!

I trust in the sincerity of your faith and your willingness; I trust in your youth; I trust in your determination to strive beyond the world of sport, for the salvation of modern man, for the coming of those "new heavens" and that "new earth" (2 Pt 3:13) for which all of us are yearning with the ardour of Christian hope.

I feel that the Church, no less than your homelands, can count on you!

You have models to inspire you. I am thinking, for example, of Pier Giorgio Frassati, who as a modern young man open to the values of sport - he was a skillful mountaineer and able skier - but at the same time he bore a courageous witness of generosity in Christian faith and charity towards others, especially the very poor and the suffering. The Lord called him to himself at only 24 years of age, in August 1925, but he is still very much alive among us with his smile and his goodness, inviting his contemporaries to the love of Christ and a virtuous life. After the First World War, he wrote the following: "Through charity, peace is sown among people; not the peace that the world gives but the true peace that only faith in Christ can give us, making us brothers and sisters." These words of his, and his spiritual friendship, I leave with you as a program, so that in every part of the world you too may be messengers of the true peace of Christ!

I hope that you will walk towards the future with that "new heart" which each of you will have been able to achieve in this Jubilee of the Redemption, as a gift of grace and a victory of love!

Amen!

VIRTUE AND CONTEMPLATION SHOULD BE YOUR DAILY FARE
(Given in Rome on April 26, 1986)

I now greet the participants in the Assembly of Delegates of the Italian Mountain Climbing Club, who are here with their General President and Central Councilors. You are all welcome to this special audience.

If it is true that sports activity, in developing and perfecting the physical and psychological potential of the person, contributes to a more complete maturity of the character, this is especially true for those who practice mountain-climbing and engage in it in respect for the ideals which this sport sustains and nourishes.

I exhort you in the words of my predecessor, Pius XII, to be "docile to the lessons of the mountain:. . .it is a lesson in spiritual elevation, of an energy which is more moral than physical" (*Discorsi e Radiomessaggi*, X pg. 219).

I congratulate you on your programs which aim at educating your members in respect for nature and in a deepened examination of the message which she imparts to the human spirit. Have special concern for the young, to train them to follow the type of life that the mountains demand of their devotees. It requires rigorous virtues in those who practice it: strict discipline and self-control, prudence, a spirit of sacrifice and dedication, care and solidarity for others. Thus we can say that mountain-climbing develops character. In fact, it would not be possible to face disinterestedly the difficulties of life on the mountains if the physical and muscular strength, which is very necessary, were not sustained by a strong will and an intelligent passion for beauty.

Help our members also to be contemplatives, to enjoy ever more deeply in their mind the message of creation. In contact with the beauties of the mountains, in the face of the spectacular grandeur of the peaks, the fields of snow and the immense landscapes, man enters into himself and discovers that the beauty of the universe shines not only in the framework of the exterior heavens, but also that of the soul that allows itself to be enlightened, and seeks to give meaning to life. From the things that it contemplates, in fact, the spirit is lifting up to God on the breath of prayer and gratitude toward the Creator.

To all of you, to the members of your club, and to all who practice the sport of mountain-climbing, I gladly impart my Blessing.

EVEN THE GREATEST CHAMPIONS NEED CHRIST
(Given in Rome on October 29, 2000 for the Jubilee for the World of Sports)

1.) "Do you not know that in a race all the runners compete, but only one receives the prize? So run that you may obtain it?" (1 Cor. 9:24).

In Corinth, where Paul had brought the message of the Gospel, there was a very important stadium where the "Isthmian Games" were held. It was appropriate then, for Paul to refer to athletic contests in order to spur the Christians of that city to push themselves to the utmost in the "race" of life. In the stadium races, he says, everyone runs, even if only one is the winner: You too run. . .With this metaphor of healthy athletic competition, he highlights the value of life, comparing it to a race not only for an earthly, passing goal, but for an eternal one. A race in which not just one person, but everyone can be a winner.

Today we are listening to these words of the Apostle as we gather in Rome's Olympic Stadium, which one again is transformed into a great open-air church, as it was for the international Jubilee for the world of sport in 1984, the Holy Year of the Redemption. Then, as it is today, it is Christ, the only Redeemer of man, who welcomes us and illumines our way with his word of salvation.

Sport can help you to develop important values

I offer a warm greeting to all of you, dear athletes and sportsmen and women from every corner of the world, who are celebrating your Jubilee! My heart-felt "thanks" to the international and Italian authorities of sport institutions, and to everyone who helped to organize this extraordinary meeting with the world of sport and its various dimensions.

I thank Mr. Juan Antonio Samaranch, president of the International Olympic Committee; Mr. Giovanni Petrucci, President of the Italian National Olympic Committee; and Mr. Giovanni Rossi, a gold medal winner at Sydney and Atlanta, for their addresses to me, expressing the sentiments of you all, dear athletes. As I look at all of you gathered in such orderly fashion in this stadium, many memories of sporting experiences in my life come to mind. Dear friends, thank you for your presence and thank you especially for the enthusiastic way you are observing this Jubilee event.

2.) With this celebration the world of sport is joining in a great chorus, as it were, to express through prayer, song, play, and movement a hymn of praise and thanksgiving to the Lord. It is a fitting occasion to *give thanks to God for the gift of sport*, in which the human person exercises his body, intellect, and will, recognizing these abilities as so many gifts of his Creator.

Playing sports has become very important today, since it can encourage young people to develop important values such as loyalty, perseverance, friendship, sharing, and solidarity. Precisely for this reason, in recent years it has continued to grow even more as one of the characteristic phenomena of the modern era, almost a "sign of the times" capable of interpreting humanity's new needs and new expectations. Sports have spread to every corner of the world, transcending differences between cultures and nations.

Because of the global dimensions this activity has assumed, those involved in sports throughout the world have a great responsibility. They are called to make sports an opportunity for meeting and dialogue, over and above every barrier of language, race, or culture. Sports, in fact, can make an effective contribution to peaceful understanding between peoples and to establishing the new civilization of love.

3.) The Great Jubilee of the year 2000 invites each and every person to engage seriously in reflection and conversion. Can the world of sport excuse itself from this providential spiritual dynamism? No! On the contrary, the importance of sports today invites those who participate in them to take this opportunity for an *examination of conscience*. It is important to identify and promote the many positive aspects of sport, but it is only right also to recognize the various transgressions to which it can succumb.

The educational and spiritual potential of sport must make believers and people of good will united and determined in challenging every distorted aspect that can intrude, recognizing it as a phenomenon opposed to the full development of the individual and to his enjoyment of life. Every care must be taken to protect the human body from any attack on its integrity, from any exploitation, and from any idolatry.

Persevering effort is needed to succeed in life

There must be a willingness to ask forgiveness for whatever has been done, or not done, in the world of sport that is in contrast to the commitments made at the last Jubilee. They will be reaffirmed in the "*Sport Manifesto*," which will be presented in a few moments. May this examination offer everyone - managers, technicians, and athletes - an opportunity to find new, creative, and motivating zeal, so that sport, without losing its true nature, can answer the needs of our time: sport that protects the weak and excludes no one, that frees young people from the snares of apathy and indifference, and arouses a healthy sense of competition in them; sport that is a factor of emancipation for poorer countries and helps to eradicate intolerance and build a more fraternal and united world; sport which contributes to the love of life, teaches sacrifice, respect, and responsibility, leading to the full development of every human person.

4.) "*Those that sow in tears shall reap rejoicing*" (Ps 125:5). The responsorial psalm reminded us that *persevering effort is needed to succeed in life*. Anyone who plays sports knows this very well: it is only at the cost of strenuous training that significant results are achieved. The athlete, therefore, agrees with the Psalmist when he says that the effort spent in sowing finds its reward in the joy of the harvest: "Although they go forth weeping, carrying the seed to be sown, they shall come back rejoicing, carrying their sheaves" (Ps 125:6).

At the recent Olympic Games in Sydney, we admired the feats of the great athletes, who sacrificed themselves for years, day after day, to achieve those results. This is *the logic of sport*, especially Olympic sports; it is also *the logic of life*: without sacrifices, important results are not obtained, or even genuine satisfaction.

Once again the Apostle Paul has reminded us on this: "Every athlete exercises self-control in all things. They do it to receive a perishable wreath, but we an imperishable" (I Cor 9:25). Every Christian is called to become a strong *athlete of Christ*, that is, a faithful and courageous witness to his Gospel. But to succeed in this, he must persevere in prayer, be trained in virtue, and follow the divine Master in everything.

He, in fact, is *God's true athlete*: Christ is the "more powerful" Man (cf. Mk 1:7), who for our sake confronted and defeated the "opponent," Satan, by the power of the Holy Spirit, thus inaugurating the kingdom of God. He teaches us that, to enter into glory, we must undergo suffering (cf. Lk 24:26, 46); he has gone before us on this path, so that we might follow in his footsteps.

Lord Jesus, help athletes to be your friends and witnesses

May the Great Jubilee help us to be strengthened and fortified to face the challenges that await us at this dawn of the third millennium.

5.) *"Jesus, Son of David, have mercy on me!"* (Mk 10:47).

These are the words of the blind man of Jericho in the Gospel episode proclaimed a few moments ago. They can also become our words: "Jesus, Son of David, have mercy on me!"

O Christ, we fix our gaze on you, who offer every person the fullness of life. Lord, you heal and strengthen those who, trusting in you, accept your will.

Today, during the Great Jubilee of the Year 2000, athletes throughout the world are gathered here in spirit, above all to renew their faith in you, man's only Saviour.

And those, like the athlete, who are at the peak of their strength, recognize that *without you, O Christ, they are inwardly like the blind man*, incapable, that is, of seeing the full truth, of understanding the deep meaning of life, especially when faced with the darkness of evil and death. Even the greatest champion finds himself defenseless before the fundamental questions of life and needs your light to overcome the demanding challenges that a human being is called to face. Lord Jesus Christ, help these athletes to be your friends and witnesses to your love. Help them to put the same effort into personal asceticism that they do into sports; help them to achieve a harmonious and cohesive unity of body and soul.

May they be sound models to imitate for all who admire them. Help them always to be athletes of the spirit, to win your inestimable prize: an imperishable crown that lasts forever. Amen!

SPORT BUILDS FRIENDSHIP AND GOODWILL
(Given in Rome on October 29, 2000)

1.) At this time of joy we cannot and must not forget that suffering and death continue in certain regions of the world. I am thinking particularly of the *Middle East region*.

Once again I wish to ask all the parties involved in the peace process to spare no efforts to restore the atmosphere of dialogue that existed until a few weeks ago. Mutual trust, rejection of weapons, and respect for international law are the only way to revive the peace process. Let us pray, therefore, for a return to the negotiating table and, through dialogue, for achieving the longed-for goal of a just and lasting peace that will guarantee everyone the inalienable right to freedom and security.

2.) We are now ready to conclude the Eucharistic celebration, the heart of this Jubilee event. We have offered sports to God as a human activity aimed at the full development of the human person and at fraternal social relations. This altar, placed in Rome's great Olympic Stadium, has reminded us that sports too are above all God's *gift*.

This gift now asks to become mission and witness. In the context of the Jubilee Year, the *"Sport Manifesto"* will shortly be read, as if to stress the concrete commitment resulting from this Jubilee.

I extend a cordial greeting to all the French-speaking athletes who are taking part in this Jubilee, and invite them to be, through sport, messengers of peace and brotherhood, as well as examples of upright and harmonioius living. With my Apostolic Blessing.

Dear English-speaking participants in this Jubilee celebration, sport has brought you together from different countries in a common interest and shared goals. Your passion for sport is a building block of human solidarity, friendship, and goodwill among peoples. May your physical exertions be a part of your quest for the higher values which build character and give you dignity and a sense of achievement, in your own eyes and in the eyes of others. In Christian terms, life itself is a contest and a striving for goodness and holiness. May God bless you in your endeavors, and may he fill you and your families with his love and peace.

I cordially greet the German-speaking athletes, coaches, and officials. The "nicest triviality in the world" is often marred by harsh competitive pressure. In all seriousness, may this thought give you serenity: even competition is just a game. Sport should be fun and enjoyable. May God's blessing go with you!

I greet the Spanish-speaking athletes. I invite you to dedicate your efforts to developing the whole person, to fostering peace among peoples and to winning the most valuable prize: receiving God's mercy and being crowned with Christ's glory.

I extend a friendly and encouraging greeting to the professional and amateur athletes from the various Portuguese-speaking countries, reminding everyone that the goal and greatest prize in life is Jesus Christ. May they never be content with less, and they will victoriously mount the podium of eternity.

I cordially greet the athletes from Poland and other countries of the world. On your Jubilee day, I join you in thanking God for the strength of spirit in which each day you spare no toil and overcome personal weakness in order to achieve your laurels in noble competition in the various disciplines of sport. Your persevering efforts and the joy of victory become a symbol to which anyone who wants to grow spiritually can appeal, particularly the Christian, who, as St. Paul says, "fights the good fight," so that once the race of life is over, he may receive from Christ's hands the "crown of righteousness" (cf. 2 Tm 4:6-7). God bless you in giving this particular witness.

3.) We now turn to Mary Most Holy, invoking her maternal protection on the entire world of sport, so that it may always be inspired by authentic values and contribute to the integral development of the human person and of society.

John Paul II, God's athlete and Mary's Pope, died on April 2, 2005 at 9:37 p.m., just as the Rosary was being prayed beneath his window in St. Peter's Square. He died on the first Saturday in honor of Mary's motherly heart and the vigil of Divine Mercy Sunday, a feast that he himself instituted on April 30, 2000. Just 90 minutes prior to his death, a Mass for Divine Mercy Sunday was celebrated in his room, and John Paul II received Communion and the anointing of the sick.

Two million people are believed to have filed past John Paul II's crimson-robed body lying in state in St. Peter's Basilica. Two hours before the funeral Mass on April 8, 2005, the Pope's body was placed in a cypress casket and closed. A document was placed in a tube and placed in the casket with the body. It read: "The whole Church, especially young people, accompanied his passing in prayer. His memory remains in the heart of the Church and of all humanity." The document highlighted themes of his pontificate such as his love for young people, his promotion of dialogue with Jews and other religions, his prayerfulness and devotion to the Rosary, and the "wisdom and courage" with which he promoted Catholic doctrine.

Cardinal Joseph Ratzinger, now Pope Benedict XVI, who

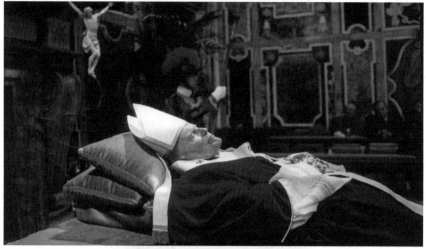

Two million people are believed to have filed past John Paul II's crimson-robed body (above) lying in state in St. Peter's Basilica on April 8, 2005. A painting of Mary embracing Lolek done by Delekta-Wincinska Iza from Krakow truly shows him to be Mary's Pope.

presided over the funeral Mass, which is considered the largest funeral in the history of the world, in his homily stated that John Paul II "offered his life for his flock and for the entire human family." He also said: "We can be sure that our beloved Pope is standing today at the window of the Father's house, that he sees us and blesses us." After the funeral, John Paul II was buried beneath St. Peter's Basilica in the grottos near St. Peter's tomb.

All sports events in Italy that weekend were suspended in tribute to the Pope. The front page of Italy's top sports newspaper read: "The time for silence." Gianni Petrucci, president of the Italian Olympic Committee, said: "For us, the sporting Pope, the athlete of athletes, has left us." Even before he was elected Pope, Cardinal Stefan Wyszynski, Archbishop of Warsaw, called him "my rugged mountaineer." Two days before the Pope died, Cardinal Theodore McCarrick of Washington, D.C. referred to his early papacy. He said: "He was filled with vim and vigor and enthusiasm. He was an athlete, a sportsman walking across the stage of the world. An Australian newspaper once described the Pope early in his papacy as "built like a rugby front-row forward. Athletes and the world of sports will truly miss this man."

John Paul II was Mary's Pope. He was the protagonist, the Bishop dressed in white, going up a steep mountain, in the story that Mary spoke about to the three children visionaries at Fatima on July 13, 1917, three years before he was born. At 5:17 p.m. on May 13, 1981, after two shots were fired at him in St. Peter's Square, John Paul II's white cassock was bloody from the waist up. The Pope would come to later say: "One hand fired the shot and another one guided the bullet." Mary's maternal hand had guided her beloved athlete throughout his life. Truly, Lolek was Mary's Pope and as a writer, it is truly an honor to dedicate this book to such a great and holy man, along with dedicating it to Mary. We will miss him, but let us remember what Cardinal Ratzinger, now Benedict XVI, said about John Paul II at his funeral: "He sees us and blesses us."

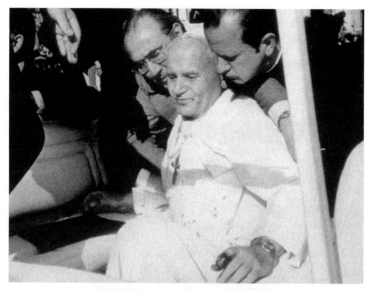

At 5:17 p.m. on May 13, 1981, shots were fired at John Paul II in St. Peter's Square (above). His cassock was bloody from the waist up. The Pope would later come to say: "One hand fired the shot and another one guided the bullet." Mary's maternal hand had guided Lolek, her beloved athlete, throughout his life.

7
Philosophy of Sport

Any philosophy of sport that would be based on and developed from a Catholic perspective would need naturally to gravitate toward John Paul II, the athlete Pope's, vision of sports and its basis on the principle of the dignity and integral development of the human person as the goal and criterion of all sporting activity. On April 12, 1984, John Paul II stated:

> But we also know what great efforts have been made to ensure that the '*philosophy of sport*' always prevails, the key principle of which is not 'sport for sport's sake' or other motives than the dignity, freedom, and integral development of man!

It is interesting to note that Pope Pius XII, the great "friend of sport," firmly believed that only a Christian philosophy of sport can effectively combat false concepts and prevent their evil influence.

On October 29, 2000, in Rome's Olympic Stadium for the Jubilee of Sports, John Paul II stated that sports are above all *God's gift*. He said at the end of Mass that we have offered sports to God as a human activity aimed at the full development of the human person. The Second Vatican Council counseled the laity to engage in temporal affairs and to direct them according to God's will; to illuminate and order all temporal things so that they may grow according to God's plan. The Catholic laity that is involved in sports and physical education in any way have a calling to give order and shed light, through a sound Christian philosophy, on the world of sport. On April 3, 1986, John Paul II told the Assembly of the Catholic Federation of Physical and Sports Education, a lay organization, that the end and measure of every sporting activity is respect for the fundamental values of the human person. He encouraged them, with God's help, to implement this philosophy and to see it as a mission. This is to be done so as to bring sports and physical education in line with God's plan, and so that sports and exercise give glory to God.

St. Paul, the Apostle to the Gentiles and an athletic person himself, taught that all things you do should be done for the glory of God. This pertains to, among other things, exercise and sports. In 1945, Pope Pius XII stated that those who accuse the Church of not caring for physical education and sports are far from the truth.

It is said that success in teaching physical education and coaching sports to the young rests more on having a sound philosophy than any other factor. A philosophy of sport would best be defined as principles and beliefs that guide our actions. Classical philosophers such as Aristotle and Aquinas help us see the role of philosophy as an examination of both our principles and beliefs. With this in mind, a philosophy of sport could help us clarify, evaluate, and adjust the principles we believe in, and to see what is needed to get them in line with the vision of exercise and sports proposed by the Magisterium of the Church - and more specifically, John Paul II. On October 29, 2000, at Rome's Olympic Stadium, Antonio Rossi, a gold medallist at both the Atlanta and Sydney Olympics, became a spokesman for all athletes. Standing before John Paul II, he said: "We promise that we will commit ourselves to live life and sports with courage, humility, and perseverance." Rossi said, quoting St. Catherine of Siena: "If you are what you are meant to be, you will set the world on fire." He told the athletes, "This motto must be our dream and objective for the new millennium."

John Paul II believed that the education and spiritual potential of sport must make believers and people of good will united in challenging every distorted aspect that can intrude upon sport, recognizing it as a phenomenon opposed to the full development of the individual and to his enjoyment of life. The Pope saw sports as becoming more and more a vital instrument for the moral

The author is seen sitting here in Athens at the Aeropagus where St. Paul preached to the people of Athens. He is collecting his thoughts for the writing of this chapter: "Philosophy of Sport." He was in Greece on assignment in April of 2005.

and spiritual elevation of the human person. The Church approves of and encourages participation in sports as a form of gymnastics of both the body and the soul, a training for social relations based on respect for one's person and respect for others. The Second Vatican Council taught that people are enriched with mutual understanding by means of physical exercise and sport, which can help to foster friendly relations between peoples of all classes, countries, and races. A sound philosophy of sport would go a long way in supplying ethical standards and principles that would help in guiding sports toward the vision that Pius XII and John Paul II had of sports.

John Paul II had clearly outlined his thoughts on exercise and sports. He believed that there needs to be an attitude of respect, esteem, and redemption for sporting activity, so that a sound philosophy of sport can be established and be beneficial. The Pope believed that when there is so much loss of hope and so much confusion today, the values enshrined in sport can open new horizons of humanism and solidarity to vast sectors of the world's young people. He encouraged leaders in various fields of sports to put their talents and leadership in the service of these values. He encouraged leaders in physical education and sports to propagate the true meaning of physical education and sports. John Paul II wonderfully expressed his conviction that athletic ability is a gift from God the Creator. He believed that sport and the healthy competition that accompanies it embodies precious gifts that can uplift a person. Pius XII's philosophy of sport was that it develops character, makes a person courageous, a generous loser, and a gracious victor; it refines the senses, gives us intellectual penetration, and steels the will to endurance. Blessed Pope John XXIII's philosophy of sport included seeing in sport and exercise gifts and advantages such as health, vigor, agility, and grace for the body and constancy, strength, and the exercise of personal sacrifice for the soul.

The Church emphasizes sport's positive value, but also realizes its negative and questionable aspects. St. Paul saw sport as an expression of man's natural faculties - that is, to be respected, but also needing correction at times and in need of redemption. John Paul II stressed that sports must not allow itself to degenerate through excessive concern for merely material advantages or through undue subordination to partisan ideologies. His philosophy was that sport is a game, a celebration, and must be properly used and freed from excess technical perfection and professionalism, being far above the harsh laws of production and consumption, and all other purely utilitarian and hedonistic considerations in life. A sound Catholic philosophy of sport can help in the correction and redemption of sport so needed in the early twenty-first century.

In a report conducted on American attitudes toward sports, 96.3 percent of the American population was found to play, watch, or read about sports. The report shows that people find being involved in sports in some way a valuable and significant activity. Sports all over the world are undergoing moral scrutiny. We hear of recruiting violations, institutions exploiting athletes, athletes not graduating at the same rate as the student population, under-the-table payments to athletes, use of performance-enhancing drugs such as anabolic steroids, and a "success at any cost" attitude that puts too much emphasis on winning. The headlines of our newspapers bring out all too well the necessity of a sound, moral philosophy of sport. One example of a coach and program that I believe exhibited a sound philosophy of team sports was John Wooden of UCLA fame, considered by many to be the greatest coach, of any sport, in American history. Winning NCAA basketball championships at UCLA was a byproduct of his sound philosophy. (I will comment on this philosophy later in this chapter.)

I think it wise to establish the foundation for a Catholic philosophy of sport with a clear understanding of the body. Pius XII's philosophy of sport was based on the fact that the body has its part to play in rendering homage to God. The materialists of today see in the body nothing but flesh, whose form, beauty, and strength bud and flower only to fade and die. The Catholic philosophy is different. The body is God's masterpiece in the order of visible creation. The Magisterium of the Church teaches us that God intends the body to flourish here below, and to enjoy immortality in the glory of heaven. Pius XII taught that the Christian philosophy of sport is to cultivate the dignity and harmony of the human body, to develop its health, agility, and grace, as it is the shrine of the Holy Spirit. This great Pope had such profound reverence and respect for the body that he taught that athletes should not ruin their health or expose their lives to danger in athletic pursuits. This would be morally illicit.

Pius XII, known as the "friend of sport," asked the question: What purpose do men run, jump, climb, walk, swim, kick, ski, fence, wrestle, cycle, and many other activities? It is the use, development, and control of the energies enclosed within the body. Pius XII believed that sport should adhere to the laws which derive from anatomy, biology, medicine, physiology, and psychology, so as to achieve the purpose of sport, which is the education, development, and strengthening of the body in its power of movement - and also that of bringing man closer to God. He taught that God formed from the slime of the earth the marvelous work which is the human body. Pius XII taught that the return to dust is not the final destiny, for it will again be called to life immortal. St. Paul taught that the body belongs to the Lord. He taught that your members are the temple of the Holy Spirit, who is in you, whom you have from God; you are not your own. Glorify God and bear Him in your body.

The Magisterium of the Church gives many motives for us to give the body the respect it deserves. Pius XII's philosophy of sport emphasizes that the greatest honor and most holy destiny of the body is its being the dwelling of a soul which radiates moral beauty and is sanctified by divine grace. Pius XII taught that it is sound to teach man to respect his body, but not more than is reasonable and right. Care of the body, strengthening of the body, but cult of the body - no. A Louis Harris poll was taken some time ago and found that 96 percent of Americans cited something about their bodies they didn't like and would change if they could. This created a boon for diet doctors, fitness advisors, plastic surgeons, and exercise clubs. Many Americans, and safe to say many all over the world, have embraced the cult of fitness to try to find meaning in life. Many people have developed the philosophy that you are how you look. Many consider sports and fitness a secular religion. The temptation today is to have competition and fitness supply the meaning of life, where God and Church were once considered the center of one's life and the way to find meaning in life. Pope Pius XII taught that only a Christian philosophy of the body and sport can effectively combat false concepts and prevent their evil influence.

In 1984 at the Olympic Stadium in Rome, John Paul II taught that the Church recommends the best use of this marvelous instrument, the body, by a suitable physical education which trains both body and soul for effort, balance, sacrifice, nobility, brotherhood, courtesy, and fair play. He taught that the Church supports physical education for all of its good and wholesome elements. John Paul II contributed to Pius XII's philosophy by teaching that sport is not merely physical power and muscular efficiency, but also soul, which must show its integral face. It is interesting to note that John Paul II saw sports as a worthwhile way of using one's time, as sports manifests an expression of the dimension of one's intelligence and will over one's body. John Paul II taught that people must be taught to see that sports are aids and accessories to be appreciated, but not the highest aim of life. What is of supreme value in life is the soul, conscience, and beyond everything else, God. John Paul II taught that if the athlete forgets the primacy of the spirit and reduces sport to the cult of the human body, letting sports hinder the moral and intellectual development, then sports would lose its true significance and would be harmful to growth as a human person. It is interesting to note that John Paul II described the true athlete as one who prepares not only by training the body but also by constantly engaging the spiritual dimensions of oneself.

To end this section on the foundation of the philosophy of the body, I would like to mention what was considered to be a main teaching of John Paul II on the body. He taught that we express ourselves through the body and enter into relationships with other persons through the body. We are called to reflect God the Trinity in our bodies. God is a trinity of persons, always self-giving. We are called to see ourselves as gifts and to offer ourselves in self-giving to God and to others. The Second Vatican Council taught that man can only find himself through a "sincere gift of self." God's intent is for the body to become a gift that is given in freedom and innocence. So first, we are all called to present our body, with the richness and resources of the masculine and feminine nature, as a living sacrifice, holy and acceptable to God. John Paul II taught us that our bodies are instruments made for union and communion, and in this we most realize our likeness to God.

In light of John Paul II's teaching on the body as a gift, I think there is a great need today for people to accept and appreciate their physical beings as God created them. God, in His goodness, has given each individual a physique, a face, nose, color of hair, etc. Each human person, made in the image and like-ness of God, is unique in every aspect of personhood, including each part, each member of the body. Today we see people dyeing their hair different colors, going to plastic surgeons, and having the shape of their nose and other areas of the body changed. Fashion magazines such as *Seventeen, Cosmopolitan, Vogue*, and *Glamour* for girls and women and *GQ* magazine for men portray a certain look that many want to emulate. Hollywood stars do their best to give the message that we are how we look. Seeking and working to cultivate the inner life, the life of grace, beauty within by a virtuous life, does not seem to have the same priority that body beautiful has in the American landscape.

I'll never forget doing research on John Wooden of UCLA fame, on whom many books have been written. On the back cover of one book he was pictured sitting, holding a basketball, and next to him on his table was a file card, in an upright position, on which was written: *"I pray thee, O God, that I may be beautiful within."* We need to cultivate the inner life today and let it be physically expressed. We need to humbly accept what God has seen good to create in each of us and not be envious of others who have a body, a look, that we would rather have.

The sports establishment would do well to realize that men and women are different, not only in body, but at the deepest psychological levels. Those in leadership positions in sport would do well to reward the physiological and psychological assets of woman by offering sport activities that enrich these assets and not denigrate them. In sports, the beauty and the richness of their femininity must be respected. A woman's resources as a person are no less than a man's, just different, such as those that are oriented toward welcoming and nurturing life.

The sports world would be wise to be watchful and vigilant over what John Paul II saw as trends in the feminist movement that seek to make woman like man. The late Pope encouraged woman not to let any situation or condition lead to the "masculinization of woman." This could easily pertain to the area of sports. The Pope encouraged women not to appropriate to themselves male characteristics contrary to their own femininity. John Paul II taught that woman's identity cannot consist in being a copy of man, since she is endowed with her own qualities and prerogatives. Sports organizations and schools would greatly be of service and help by encouraging sport activity that enriches the feminine qualities and not denigrate or diminish what is characteristic of woman, of what is feminine.

Another area that needs to be mentioned is modesty. The Church teaches that modesty means refusing to unveil parts of the body that should remain hidden. Modesty inspires one's choice of clothing. It makes it possible to resist the allurements of fashion and the pressures of prevailing ideologies. Pius XII was very astute in his time in observing the need for modesty. He taught that just as there are sports which, by their austerity, help to keep the instincts in check, so too there are other forms of sport that reawaken them, either by sensual allurement or by violent pressure. Pius XII taught that in certain sports there is an immodesty which is neither necessary nor proper. The religious and moral sense places its veto on this improper attire. The Church teaches that by making people aware of modesty, it awakens in them respect for the human person, and also awakens consciousness of being a subject worthy of dignity and respect, not an object to be exploited. Pius XII taught that sports should not command and control, but serve and help. This is their duty, and it is in serving and helping that they find reason for their existence. All this amounts to standing up to the prevailing culture and ideologies and expressing our character by making a stand on our beliefs. It was John Wooden of UCLA who said: "Sports not only builds character, but reveals it." He always taught that having beliefs and standing up for them goes straight to the issue of character.

Another topic I believe needs discussion and thought in order to establish a sound philosophy of sport is the emphasis on winning in sports. A very important principle to consider is what John Paul II told athletes in Rome's Olympic Stadium in 2000: "The 'nicest triviality in the world' is often marred by harsh competitive pressure. May this thought give you serenity: even competition is just a game. Sport should be fun and enjoyable" (*L'Osservatore Romano*, November 1, 2001, p. 2). The Pope told the athletes in Rome on October 29, 2000 that your physical exertions should be a part of your quest for the high values which build character and give you dignity and a sense of achievement in your eyes and in the eyes of others. This statement can be the starting point for a very healthy and thoughtful consideration and the ground work for a sound philosophy in sports.

Cardinal George Pell, Archbishop of Sydney, Australia, was once offered a professional contract to play Australian rules football, which he excelled at. He decided rather to study to become a priest. His long list of athletic accomplishments includes playing basketball, tennis, rugby, cricket, track and field, swimming, and rowing crew. His coaching experiences included soccer, crew, and Australian rules football. This great sportsman states:

> Where others promote winning at any cost, the Church teaches the great virtues such as temperance, courage, justice, hope, faith, and speaks up for human character that is based upon these qualities. Where individualism reigns, the Church proposes communal effort and social responsibilities, while safeguarding the individual's rights. Where play and sport are reduced to winnings or contaminated by drugs, the Church reminds us that the prize in the only race that ultimately matters is eternal life and that cheats compromise their honor and their chances of ultimate happiness.

John Wooden of UCLA never mentioned winning or losing for the 27 years he was at that university (1948-75). He always urged his basketball players to strive to become the best of which they were capable. Total effort was the measurement he used, not the final score. In Steve Jamison's book titled *Wooden*, he mentions that for John Wooden, the question was not "Did I win?" or "Did I lose?" Those are the wrong questions. The correct question is: "Did I make my best effort?" That's what matters. The rest of it gets in the way. John Wooden had a record setting 10 NCAA basketball national championships in 12 years at UCLA. He had an 88-game winning streak and has been considered by many to be the greatest coach in American history. He has been hailed by many as "the greatest coach of the twentieth century." He was awarded the *Presidential Medal of Freedom*, America's highest civilian award, by President George Bush in 2003. And all this from a man who never mentioned winning. In Steve Jamison's other book on John Wooden, titled *My Personal Best*, he states Wooden's philosophy: "Try your hardest. Make the effort. Do your best. The score can't make you a loser when you do that; it can't make you a winner if you do less" (p. 6). It is not that Wooden did not want his players to work to win, but he tried to convince them that they had always won when they had done their best. Jamison also states in his book that John Wooden defined success in the following way: "Success is peace of mind which is a direct result of self-satisfaction in knowing you did your best to become the best that you are capable of becoming" (p. 6). For John Wooden, success is 100 percent of your effort to the struggle. He developed the Pyramid of Success, which was a combination of personal qualities and values that are important in making the effort to reach your potential. They include: industriousness, friendship, loyalty, cooperation, enthusiasm, self-control, alertness, initiative, intentness, condition, skill, team spirit, poise, confidence, competitive greatness, patience, and faith.

He believed that character was central for a player to be a team player. He believed that sports show that you must think of the group as a whole rather than just of yourself as an individual. He believed it important to let all the players on the team know that they are valued and appreciated. He believed that every player deserved to be valued and feel valued. He also firmly believed that if you discipline yourself, others won't have to.

John Wooden always wanted his players at UCLA to honor God by doing their best and controlling their emotions. He believed that winning scores and great reputations are meaningless in the eyes of God, because God knows what we really are and that is all that matters. He learned from Mother Teresa, one of his two favorite teachers, that a life not lived for others is not a life. He was a coach of great self-giving. He always encouraged his players to be unselfish and to play for the good of the team and not for individual glory. He believed that coaches who are committed to the Christ-like life will be helping the young to develop wholesome disciplines of body, mind, and spirit that will build character worthy of God's calling.

For John Wooden, winning was second to developing the character of his players. Character and integrity of the individual is what he aimed at in developing his athletes. He believed that one should be more concerned with character than reputation, because your character is what you really are, while your reputation is merely what others think you are. He never measured success in sports by trophies. For him, the highest success is your personal best. For him, being a coach or a teacher meant helping your players or students to be better people, and in this John Wooden truly gave it his personal best. I firmly believe that John Wooden's philosophy of life and sport is truly in line with that of Pius XII and John Paul II, Popes who were known to be "friends of sport."

In many ways, America is obsessed with success and winning in sports. What importance should be assigned to winning in athletic competition? The 1896 Olympic Creed, written by Pierre de Combertin, was: "Not in the winning but in the taking part. Not in the conquering but in the fighting." Knute Rockne of Notre Dame fame was asked, "How do you think the season went?" He responded by telling the person who asked to check back with him in 10 or 15 years. Then he would know what kind of young men he had produced and what kind of citizens they had become.

Only judging by that standard could he be able to evaluate the season.

Rainer Martens, Ph.D., founder of the American Sports Education Program, the largest coaching education program in the United States, believes that it's not how many games you win, but how many young people you help to become winners in life. His philosophy is: "athletes first, winning second." He and his program challenge coaches to ask themselves if playing only their best athletes is putting the athletes on the team first. In a society that puts so much value on winning, coaches must ask themselves if they reflect more concern for winning than for the development of the athletes. Many coaches in a society that rewards winning have to look at their objectives in coaching, because they are often judged on their win-loss record. So often, coaches are conditioned or pressured by the organization for whom they coach to pursue winning at all costs. Coaches and A.D.s who adhere to the philosophy of "athletes first, winning second" must stick to their principles when pressure to win threatens their jobs or self-worth. Today, society seems to reward winning more than developing young people's character.

Coaches who want to implement a Christian perspective in their objectives must be in the forefront of this coaching philosophy of putting "athletes first, winning second." Their decision and behavior must reflect their philosophy of doing what is best for their athletes, and secondly, doing what may improve their team's chances of winning. Athletic directors who adhere to this philosophy must support their coaches and give them guidance in this area. A.D.s can easily reverse this philosophy and put winning first, athletes second. The temptation is for A.D.s to replace coaches who do not have winning records. John Paul II firmly believed that sports can lose its real objective when it leaves room for other interests that ignore the central character of the human person.

The philosophy of "athletes first, winning second" does not mean that athletes do not strive to win according to the rules of the game. Striving to win is part of enjoyable and fun competition. It is the short term objective of any game. But striving to win is never as important as the well-being of the athlete. This is not to say that the pursuit of victory is not important, as the longing for or the pursuit of victory is fun. According to John Wooden, it is not that winning is not valued, but the emphasis is in doing your best.

A code of ethics or behavior for coaches as well as for athletes and parents will be considered in this chapter on the philosophy of sport. Something that John Wooden learned from his father when he was young was "know thyself." This is a principle that will go a long way in helping those in leadership positions in sports. When you are at peace with yourself, you can help athletes be at peace with themselves. One thing coaches know instinctively is that the young look for role models. Self-esteem in a coach is very important. It is your inner conviction about your competency and worth as a human being. We really can't base our self-esteem on winning or losing, because they are not under our control. If you feel worthy as a person, you will recognize worth in others. How we relate to ourselves affects how we relate to others and the world around us.

Many experts in sports believe that competition in sports can help the young develop morally by being on a team that has established a code of ethics. This is where the coach comes in and sees to it that there is a set of rules that everyone is accountable to. The coach can set the atmosphere. John Wooden used to tack mottos and phrases on bulletin boards, such as: "Discipline yourself and others won't have to" and "The best way to improve your team is to improve yourself." It has been said that the end purpose of discipline is the development of the human person who respects self, other persons, and those in authority. John Wooden's philosophy was that you must have respect for those under your supervision. Then they will do what you ask and more. He always believed in being reasonable with his players and treating them fairly.

The code of ethics the coach sets for his players can be transferred to a moral code for life. Five moral values that are supported by character educators are:

1.) Be respectful

2.) Be responsible
3.) Be caring
4.) Be honest
5.) Be fair.

Playing according to the rules and not cheating can go a long way in helping develop a life based on the Ten Commandments and the Eight Beatitudes. Pope Pius XII once asked athletes the question: "Do you wish to act rightly in sports? Then keep the Ten Commandments."

Code of ethics for coaches

1.) Coaches are to be careful not to achieve personal objectives at the expense of the athletes.

2.) Coaches are to implement the philosophy that character education is where sports should be directed.

3.) Coaches are to be models of sportsmanship, showing respect for the game, coaches, athletes, and officials. Knute Rockne once said" "One man practicing sportsmanship is far better than 50 others preaching it."

4.) Coaches will treat athletes with respect and be fair and reasonable.

5.) Coaches are to take an active role in the prevention of drug, alcohol, and tobacco abuse. They are to communicate that performance-enhancing drugs such as anabolic steroids and other agents violate the rules, constitutes cheating, and is harmful to your health. In 2003 the *Centers for Disease Control* stated in their findings that 1 in 16 high school students reported having used steroids, up from 1 in 27 in 1999.

6.) Coaches are to provide settings that are suitable and safe. They are to abstain from training methods that are harmful. They are to consider the health of athletes in all situations.

7.) Coaches are to combine sincere praise for positive accomplishment, along with constructive criticism. John Wooden of UCLA used discipline to correct and improve, not to embarrass or ridicule.

8.) Coaches are to monitor all practices and make them safe, reasonable, and fair. John Wooden was asked if he missed coaching games at UCLA. He said: "No - I miss the practices." He believed that the glory is in getting there. He believed that practice is where champions are created.

9.) Coaches are to make sports fun and enjoyable and encourage teamwork. John Wooden would never tolerate players seeking individual glory, but to play for the good of the team. John Paul II taught that sports should be a fun and enjoyable activity for the young.

Code of ethics for athletes

John Paul II taught that athletes are often in the public eye and that they have a responsibility to set high standards of sportsmanship and personal excellence.

1.) Athletes are to be unselfish, always playing for the good of the team and never seeking individual glory.

2.) The true athlete is to have character and not be a character always seeking attention.

3.) Athletes are to give 100 percent of their effort to the struggle. The winning is in doing your best. They are never to cease trying to be the best they can be, always striving for their personal best.

4.) Based on Gospel principles, athletes are to:
-- be honest and committed to integrity
-- win graciously and lose with dignity
-- be respectful and courteous toward others
-- demonstrate good sportsmanship.
-- prepare themselves not only by training their bodies, but also by constantly engaging the spiri tual dimensions of their being. Perhaps reading chapter 10 will help.

Archbishop Timothy Dolan of Milwaukee states:

Athletics have always been an effective

school of discipleship. Traits valuable in sports . . . fairness, honor, valor, development of God-given talent, and teamwork . . . can all become virtues in the greatest 'race of all: to get to heaven."

Cardinal George Pell, Archbishop of Sydney, states:

Sports and exercise are parts of life in which we can strive for goals and for victory in peace and with respect for each other. This is obviously preferable to victory through violence or through dishonesty and unfairness. Where sport is clean, open, friendly, and from a position of rough equality, individuals, and especially young-sters, benefit enormously.

Code of ethics for parents

1.) Be supportive of your child's being on a team. Don't try to relive your athletic experience through your child. Don't pressure your child.

2.) Keep winning in perspective and help your child to give his or her personal best. In that way, your child will always be a winner, win or lose. Show your child that you appreciate his or her effort.

3.) Help your child to have fun and enjoy athletic experi-ences. Help your child to set realistic performance goals, accord-ing to ability.

4.) Don't coach your child during the game. Let the coach be the coach.

5.) Get to know the coach's philosophy and attitudes so that you gladly place your child under his guidance.

6.) Be in control of your emotions at the game, so as not to draw attention to yourself and embarrass your child.

7.) Help your child train for spiritual fitness and holiness as well, by a life of prayer, receiving the sacraments, knowing the faith, and witnessing to it. Perhaps reading chapter 10 will help.

I hope this chapter will help to correct false concepts and

their evil influences, as Pius XII taught that only a Christian philosophy of sport can combat them. He taught that the Catholic ideal will always be a safeguard of enlightenment for the place sports have in human life, the family, and the community. I also hope that this chapter will help the philosophy of sport prevail that promotes the dignity and the integral development of man that John Paul II had so hoped for and promoted.

8
Benefits of Exercise

Our bodies are temples of the Holy Spirit. The Church teaches us that the body is the masterpiece of God's creation. The Father of the Church, Clement of Alexandria, encouraged us to make an effort to be healthy, along with being holy. He valued exercise very much as benefiting health and aiding in the wholesome development of character. St. Paul encourages us to cultivate the dignity and harmony of our body. St. Thomas Aquinas considered taking care of the body through exercise as virtue and wisdom. He considered exercise as medicine for the soul. Aquinas has helped the Church reconstruct the view of exercise as a means for perfecting the body as an instrument of the mind in its search for and communication of the truth. One of the benefits of exercise that John Paul II had commented on is the power of concentration that is developed. He had also commented on exercise developing discipline. The Church encourages exercise as a means to develop self-control and discipline, which, along with God's grace and prayer, will help us in the battle to be chaste in our state of life.

1. Long ago, Hippocrates said, "Exercise strengthens while inactivity wastes."

Hypokinetic diseases, which refer to a disease or condition related to or caused by a lack of regular physical exercise, are all too prevalent today. Cardinal George Pell, Archbishop of Sydney, Australia, states:

> How many of us waste our leisure by turning personal comfort into a life of indolence or inactivity? Where life is easy, it is tempting to become lazy, slothful, to lose aspirations, fail to expand horizons, or make connections with other people - in short, it is tempting to stop being active.

Heart disease accounts for nearly one-half of all deaths in the U.S. The United States has the highest death rate from cardiovascular disease of any nation in the world. Hans Kraus, M.D. and Kenneth Cooper, M.D., have in their medical careers demonstrated how exercise and sports can help in the prevention of hypokinetic disease.

2. The American College of Sports Medicine gives us good reasons to exercise in order to remain healthy.

Some of the reasons are:

a.) Exercise increases the amount of blood your heart can pump

b.) It lowers the heart rate when the body is at rest.

c.) It improves levels of cholesterol in the blood

d.) It lowers blood pressure

e.) It reduces body fat

f.) It helps manage stress

g.) It helps you feel more energetic

h.) It helps you sleep better

i.) It helps your self-image. The Church Father, Clement of Alexandria, taught that exercise improves your complexion and improves your figure and personal appearance.

A further development of some of these benefits could be helpful in motivating us to exercise. Aerobic exercise, such as brisk walking, running, swimming, bicycle riding, done continually for at least 20 minutes, strengthens the heart, the pump of life. The heart is a muscle that beats on the average of 72 beats a minute, and 100,000 beats a day, circulating 2,000 gallons of blood a day through 60,000 miles of blood vessels.

Exercise increases the size and strength of the heart. It increases the total blood volume being pumped per beat to the cells of the body. It also causes a reduction in the resting heart rate. This slower heart rate and increased stroke volume creates a greater rest for the heart between beats. Studies have shown that people who exercise have a lower resting blood pressure than people who do not exercise. Exercise lowers the concentration of fat in the blood, which can block the coronary arteries, causing a heart attack. Another benefit of exercise for the heart is that it enlarges blood vessels and also increases the number of red blood cells, thereby increasing the capacity to carry oxygen to the cells of the body.

Aerobic exercise increases the amount of oxygen we take into our system. The smallest unit of the body is the cell; groups of cells joined together are called tissues and combinations of different kinds of tissues form organs. Each of the cells of our body needs a sufficient supply of oxygen. We need energy in all the processes of life, and this needed energy is produced in the cells by chemical reactions which consume oxygen. Oxygen being supplied to body tissues is the basis of conditioning. We need oxygen for our heart, brain, and other organs. We can live for weeks without food, but hardly five to twelve minutes without oxygen. Muscles burn energy and call on the heart and lungs to deliver oxygen-rich blood to them. This same blood returns with carbon dioxide which it expels into the lungs. A muscle without a proper oxygen supply will contract a few hundred times before starting to fatigue.

We get oxygen from the lungs, which receive it from the air we breathe. We assimilate about 21 percent oxygen from the air we breathe. Ernst Van Aaken, M.D., a European doctor, in his work on sports medicine and physical fitness has demonstrated that while sedentary we take in 6-10 liters of air per minute, with 12-20 breaths assimilating one-quarter of a liter of oxygen per minute from this air. In endurance exercise such as light running or bicycle riding, done continuously for a half hour and at a heart rate of between 130-150 beats per minute, we assimilate 2-3 liters of oxygen per minute from the 50-60 liters of air that we breathe in. Dr. Van Aaken encourages endurance activity that at a minimum causes us to assimilate 1 ½-2 liters of oxygen per minute.

Another benefit of exercise is that it increases the rate at which enzymes in the muscles pick up oxygen from the blood. Exercise also strengthens the intercostals muscles (located between the ribs). The increased strength of the intercostals muscles increases the size of the chest cavity, allowing more air to enter into the lungs with each breath, thus increasing our oxygen supply.

3. Exercise relieves tension from muscles and helps us to relax.

In our everyday life we are affected by many interior and exterior irritations and annoyances - personal problems, traffic jams, the ring of the telephone, the loud noises of the radio or television. When our bodies get ready to respond to an irritation or challenge, our muscles get tense, adrenaline pours into our system, our heart beats faster, we breathe quicker, and our blood pressure rises. Exercise as a means of releasing tension and bringing rest and regenerating a tired mind was part of St. Thomas Aquinas's philosophy.

Underexercised muscles never get a chance to get rid of tension. A muscle shortens with tension and this tension prohibits muscular relaxation. A muscle must relax as part of its function, and if it does not relax, it stays tight. With activity, there are small changes in the electrical activity within the muscle. Electromyographic (EMG) instruments can indicate levels of nervous tension by measuring the degree of electrical changes in the muscle, the principle being that the more electrical impulses in the muscles, the higher the tension level is. Studies have shown that after exercise, the electrical activity in the muscles is lower. Aerobic and therapeutic exercises release tension, making the muscles more flexible and resilient.

The increased amount of adrenaline in the blood due to constant irritation tends to tighten and restrict muscles of the body. Vigorous exercise can help break excess adrenaline and lessen the detrimental effects of adrenaline produced by emotional stress. Many psychiatrists recommend physical activity and sports for tension relief. Many of them believe that exercise and sports serve better than the pills as a tranquilizer for the release of tension. Ronald M. Lawrence, M.D., Ph.D., noted in the field of sports medicine and physical fitness, asserts that as you do aerobic exercise your brain produces endorphins, a hormone that helps in relieving nervous tension and aids in relaxation. William Menninger, M.D., a psychiatrist and founder of the Menninger Clinic in Topeka, Kansas, encouraged physical activity as an outlet for instinctive aggressive drives by enabling a person to "blow off steam," thus providing relaxation and being a supplement for daily work.

4. Aerobic exercise provides psychological benefits.

Many reports have indicated that as you exercise, you bring in more oxygen to your brain, and this makes you more alert and attentive. Ray Killinger, M.D., a psychiatrist, in his report on aerobic exercise has indicated that:

> Aerobic fitness results in improvement in the following categories of the thinking process: originality of thought, duration of concentration, mental response time, ability to change topics and subjects quickly, depth of thinking, duality of thought - the ability to entertain a number of ideas at once, and finally, mental tenacity.[51]

Kenneth Cooper, M.D., M.Ph., of the Aerobics Center in Dallas, Texas, is convinced that being physically fit can definitely help in being psychologically fit. In studies conducted at his Clinic and Institute for Aerobic Research, exercise has shown to help people better able to handle stress, gain in feelings of well-being, and help in reducing depression. Dr. Cooper attests to the conviction that aerobic exercise helps people in improving their self-image, and along with improved self-image, become more confident and outgoing. John Paul II saw exercise as a means for the body to reach optimum condition, which he taught will bring marked consequences and psychological well-being.

Robert S. Brown, M.D., a psychiatrist at the University of Virginia, and Keith Johnsgard, Ph.D., author of the book, *The Exercise Prescription for Depression and Anxiety*, both believe that running, brisk walking, swimming, and bicycling may definitely be the best prescription for mild depression. In his book, Keith Johnsgard, a clinical psychologist, cites numerous case study examples of how exercise has been useful in the treatment of both anxiety and mood disorders in his patients. As noted in his book, Johnsgard notes that research continually shows that 30 minutes of aerobic exercise three times a week will significantly reduce depression. In his book, Johnsgard states: "In all of my years on the trails of roadways, I have never seen depressed walkers" (p. 166).

Dr. Brown finds that aerobic exercise works better than pills in controlling moderate depression. Dr. Malcolm Carruthers and a medical team from England reported that as little as 10 minutes of endurance exercise can double the body's level of norepinephrine, a neuro-hormone that is associated with alertness and feeling joyous. Researchers claim that stress lowers norepinephrine levels in the brain, whereas exercise tends to increase norpinephrine in the brain. Depressed people are known to be low in norepinephrine. A number of studies have examined the role of exercise in preventing mental illness and promoting and maintaining mental health. Research has been conducted since the late 1960s and presents evidence for the beneficial effects of exercise on depression, both clinical and non-clinical. Findings indicate that physical activity is to be associated with better mental health, including fewer symptoms of depression and anxiety. Studies also show an association between lack of activity and depression and people who are less active or sedentary are at greater risk for depression than are people who are more active. The increasing presence of mental health problems in the industrialized nations has led many investigators to suggest the decline of physical activity is largely responsible for the rise of mental health concerns. The publication *The Physician and Sportsmedicine* conducted a survey which revealed that of 1,750 physicians who participated in the survey, 85 percent prescribed exercise for patients suffering from depression.

As you do aerobic exercise, endorphins are produced, which are morphine-like substances which are produced by the brain and pituitary gland to aid the body in resisting pain. Ronald M. Lawrence, M.D., Ph.D., of UCLA's Neuropsychiatric Institute and noted in the field of sports medicine and physical fitness, asserts that "endorphins help you learn and remember, counteract depression, relax you and relieve nervous tension, and make it easier for you to sleep soundly at night."[52] Dr. Lawrence asserts that "the more you exercise, the more endorphins you manufacture and the better you feel"[53]. He thinks that endorphins could be the source of the "runner's high" that runners talk about.

In all the literature that pertains to the psychological benefits of exercise, there is a consensus that exercise does produce an improved sense of well-being. This sense of well-being is attributed to such things as a decrease in anxiety, stress, and energy. Literature in this area also attests to the ancient Greek notion that a sound body ensures a sound mind.

5. Exercise helps to control obesity.

Obesity has become a problem for many in the United States in the past few decades. Obesity can cause many complications, such as heart, respiratory, kidney, and gall bladder diseases, along with diabetes and disorders of bones and joints. Regular exercise, especially aerobic exercise, is one of the keys to losing excess body fat, increasing lean body mass, and maintaining a balanced metabolism.

Aerobic exercise raises your basal or resting metabolic rate for between six and eighteen hours, so you will continue to burn extra calories long after you finish your exercise, even when you are sleeping. Aerobic exercise and restriction of caloric intake reduces fat; whereas people who go on a diet without exercise tend to often lose muscle tissue, and if they do lose fat, they usually regain it after the diet is over. Exercise not only burns fat but also tones and firms muscles.

Exercise can help you burn more calories than you take in, and this can help lose excess fat. In most cases, inactivity is the cause of obesity. Harvard's Dr. Jean Mayer, well-known scientist and nutritionist, has stated that he is convinced that inactivity is the most important factor explaining the frequency of creeping overweight in modern societies.

Even though we need a certain percentage of fat, excess fat can lead to diseases such as diabetes, coronary artery disease, and high blood pressure. In general, men should try to keep their fat weight at less than 16 to 19 percent of their total body weight, whereas women should maintain it at under 22 percent. An expert would evaluate a subject's physique by measuring skin-fold thickness with calipers, or by the more exact method of hydrostatic underwater weighing.

Aerobic exercise gives the muscles time to burn off fat, whereas bursts of energy called anaerobic exercise tends to burn glucose for fuel instead of fat. The areas of the body you should see a decrease in body fat are the abdomen, thighs, buttocks, and hips. Research has found that swimming does not produce the desired effect of losing body fat. It is better to do aerobic exercises such as running, bicycle riding, stationary bike, cross-country skiing, or brisk walking. Sit-ups done for losing body fat in the abdomen does not produce the desired effect.

Exercise is used to change muscle chemistry so that we burn fat more efficiently. Covert Baily, author of *Fit or Fat,* asserts that aerobic exercise produces a growth of fat-burning enzymes in your muscles. He recommends that aerobic exercise be done continuously for at least 12 minutes at a pace that enables you to go as fast as you can without getting out of breath or feeling exhausted when you finish. He recommends a heart rate 60 to 85 percent of your maximum heart rate while you exercise. Studies have found that vigorous, continuous aerobic exercise tends to reduce the appetite, and that is why some fitness experts recommend brisk walking, running, stationary bike or bicycling before dinner.

6. Exercise, depending on the type, increases size, strength, and endurance of muscles.

Aerobic exercise, because of the efficient delivery of oxygen and removal of waste products, increases the endurance of muscles, allowing them to work longer without getting fatigued. Weight training and calisthenics causes an increase of strength in the muscles due to a thickening of the sarcolemma of the muscle fibers. The amount of connective tissue within the muscle also thickens. The size of the muscle fibers are increased due to exercise. Exercise also causes an increased blood flow into the muscle tissue, resulting in an increase in the size of the muscle. Exercise causes an increase of capillaries, thus providing better circulation of blood to the muscle.

7. Vigorous exercise makes your bones grow in size, thickness, and strength.

There are 206 bones in the normal adult body. Aerobic exercise and other exercise that moves your body against gravity makes bones grow in size, thickness, and strength. Exercise can protect people against bone deterioration known as osteoporosis. Brisk walking is excellent for the hips and spine.

8. Exercise is also known to keep the digestive and excretory organs in good shape.

Exercise helps the muscles and nerves of the stomach and intestines become well toned and improves their ability to work in an efficient manner.

9

Guidelines for an Individual and Family Exercise Program

The foundation for an individual exercise program is a medical evaluation to obtain clearance for a program of exercises. Adults and even the young would be wise to invest in a medical evaluation prior to participating in competitive sports. An exercise prescription which provides the proper dosage should be given according to an individual's age, level of fitness, ability, disability, likes, and dislikes. As early as the third century, Clement of Alexandria, a Church Father whose main concerns were keeping healthy and becoming holy, taught that one should carefully select exercises, as each individual person has different needs. A professionally trained expert such as an exercise physiologist, physical education teacher, physical therapist, or a sports medicine professional can help with an individualized prescription of exercise. This help can prevent problems that arise when people do not recognize their own limitations, thereby going beyond a safe level of exercise.

When we think of exercise in terms of prescription and proper dosage, we remember St. Thomas Aquinas' view of exercise as medicine for the soul and regeneration for the fatigued mind.

Parents need to be concerned with their children's aerobic

fitness. The National Children and Youth Fitness study reported that one-third of all youth ages 10 to 18 did not exercise enough to give them any aerobic health-related benefits. A study sponsored by the AAU and Chrysler Corporation found that only 32 percent of children ages 6 to 17 meet minimal standards for cardio-vascular fitness, flexibility, upper body strength, and abdominal strength.

The Fathers of the Second Vatican Council stressed the role of parents as the primary educators of their children. It is best for parents to start out by being examples of fitness for their children, and by giving them opportunities to improve their fitness and motor skills so as to achieve a level of athletic achievement according to their developmental age and interest. Children need to be offered opportunities that will develop their health and character instead of being offered television and video games as after-school activities. Family fitness activities that are fun and enjoyable can be helpful in improving communication among family members.

EXERCISE PRESCRIPTION

When considering a program of exercise, attention should be given to 1) type of activity, 2) intensity of activity, and 3) duration and frequency of activity.

TYPES OF ACTIVITY

Individuals or families should select activities and exercises that they enjoy and that are suited to their present fitness level. It is important to gradually get in shape, adapting your body to regular exercise. It is best to view exercise and sports as a lifetime project - one that will need our perseverance and motivation. Pope John Paul II had remarked that individuals who care for their body and make good use of the body through exercise and sports will benefit from the marked consequences of psychological well-being. He has also remarked that we can develop through long hours of exercise and effort the power of concentration and the habit of discipline.

An exercise program should place primary emphasis on aerobic exercise that is undertaken for health-related benefits. Muscular strength, muscular endurance, and flexibility are also important and should be integrated into one's exercise program. Aerobic exercise develops cardiorespiratory endurance. The word aerobic is derived from two Greek words meaning "life" and "air." Activities that increase fresh supplies of oxygen and done for prolonged periods (at least 20 minutes) are called aerobic. We develop endurance and a strong will through these activities. Pope Pius XII viewed exercise as a way of tempering the character and forming the will as hard as steel.

As far as aerobic activities for children under age 10 are concerned, it is recommended that parents emphasize aerobic play such as: tag, chase, hide and seek, and random running instead of the regular 20 minutes or more of continuous vigorous activity.

Aerobic activities that use large muscle groups that are rhythmical and maintained continuously are:

Brisk walking: Walking is a natural exercise, one that is recommended for beginners, for those who have not exercised for some time, and even for the fittest. Walking is nonjarring, making it less likely to cause injury. Besides aerobic and weight control benefits, people who start their exercise program with walking tend to stick with it and not give up. Walking is known to be an excellent way to build strong bones and help prevent osteoporosis.

For those who have been sedentary, it is best to begin with a 10-minute walk, then add 5 minutes to your walk until you are walking for 30-45 minutes per outing. For some, walking is a way of preparing for more vigorous activity such as jogging, biking, and swimming. For others, they are content for walking to be their main exercise activity. Good shoes are essential for walking. Running shoes or shoes designed for exercise walking are recommended.

We read of the saints of the Middle Ages being great walkers, walking across Europe - especially St. Dominic, the great preacher of the Rosary, described by his contemporaries as the "strong athlete." His vigorous nature and physical energy, aided by God's grace, strengthened him to be morally fit and robust in the interior, spiritual life. St. Thomas Aquinas is known to have walked 9,000 miles during his lifetime. In the 1700s, St. Louis de Montfort, the great teacher of the Rosary and one who was a very powerful and strong man, walked 18,000 miles during his lifetime.

Jogging/Running: For beginners, for those who are sedentary, out of shape, or overweight, they should use walking as the primary means of getting in shape before they begin jogging or running. When you do start jogging, start out walking for five minutes, then a slow jog for five minutes, alternating these two movements. This can be done for the first three to four weeks, until you can comfortably jog without discomfort. Observing good running form is essential. Keep the hands and shoulders relaxed, head up, and make sure you do not run on the balls of your feet, but in more of a flat-footed stride. Good running shoes are crucial. If you have a history of orthopedic problems or health problems, or have been sedentary for some time, it is best to seek medical clearance before starting a running routine.

Swimming: Swimming is a most popular sport in America. As well as providing aerobic benefits, swimming is excellent for developing muscle strength and muscle endurance. It puts less stress on the joints, ligaments, and tendons than do other activities, due to the natural buoyancy of water.

It is important to learn how to swim efficiently using different strokes and in learning to breathe properly. The crawl (or freestyle), backstroke, breaststroke, and sidestroke are great for developing your shoulder, chest, back, leg, and arm muscles. The sidestroke is great for warming up and for slowing and cooling down. It is best to gradually work up to doing continuous laps by taking rests as needed between laps. Many recommend getting in shape by walking or riding a stationary bike before taking on a swimming routine, and, as with other activities, medical clearance is advised. Pope Piux XII was an avid swimmer, and Pope John

Paul II is known to have been very fond of swimming.

Cycling: Outdoor recreational cycling is an excellent means of aerobic conditioning and weight loss. Because of the bike seat supporting much of your weight, there is less stress on your joints than in jogging or running. For beginners, those out of shape, it is best to build up gradually, perhaps 10 minutes a day, then adding on 5 minutes per week. Be sure to pedal with the balls of your feet, not your insteps or heels. It is important to find the right seat height to avoid knee pain. This is done by sitting on the seat with your legs extended and the ball of your foot resting on the pedal at the bottom of the pedal stroke position. There should be only a slight bend (10 to 15 degrees) in the knee - adjust your seat accordingly. The indoor stationary bike is also an excellent way of exercising. It is great for when it is too wet or too hot outside. You get the same benefits as from outdoor cycling, except for the scenery, sunshine, and fresh air. Be sure to check the proper seat height, just as you do with outdoor cycling. It is advised to get medical clearance if you have health problems, or are really out of shape, before taking on cycling.

Excellent resource books for aerobic activities and fitness are: *The Aerobics Way* by Kenneth Cooper, M.D., M.Ph. (M. Evans and Company, Inc.) and *The Aerobics Program for Total Well-Being* by Kenneth Cooper, M.D., M.Ph. (Bantam Books).

Musculoskeletal conditioning activities that develop muscular strength and endurance are:

Calisthenics: These are isotonic exercises that use our own body weight for resistance. Muscular fitness involves two health-related components: strength and muscular endurance. Strength helps in doing more work at one time, to move more easily, and in developing good posture. Muscular endurance helps you to keep on working at a given activity. Children are very deficient in both of these areas. Calisthenics can help develop both components. They can also help us in resisting fatigue, prevent back problems, and help in enjoying recreational and sport activities without injury. Children seven years old or under are recommended to use playgroup apparatus to develop strength and endurance. For minimal fitness, three days a week is encouraged. Two basic calisthenics are push-ups and sit-ups.

Push-ups: These are excellent for developing strength and endurance in the upper body. A study by the American Athletic Union found that 40 percent of boys and 70 percent of girls can do only one push-up.

Procedure: The recommended way of doing a push-up is to lie on your stomach on the floor with your hands palms down on the ground, about shoulder width apart. With your toes on the ground and your back and legs straight, push slowly upward until your arms are fully extended, then lower yourself to the ground. Gradually work yourself up to doing 10 to 20 push-ups for minimal fitness. You can then try doing two or three sets of 10-20 push-ups each, with rests between sets. Youngsters and adults who are beginners are recommended to start off with modified push-ups. These are done the same way, except that you keep your knees on the ground. Be sure you do not hyperextend your back - keep your back straight.

Sit-ups: These are excellent for developing abdominal muscles. Low back pain is a major problem in the U.S. It is reported that 80 percent of low back problems result from lack of flexibility in the back and hamstring muscles, and poor posture, which results from weak abdominal muscles. Strong stomach muscles can help prevent the forward tilt of the pelvis, which can cause pain. Dr. Hans Kraus, author of the book *Hypokinetic Disease*, reported that 25 percent of all U.S. youngsters cannot do a single sit-up because of weak abdominal muscles.

Procedure: The proper way to do a sit-up is to lie on your back with knees bent, with your heels about 15 inches from your buttocks. Cross your arms in front of your chest, with hands holding opposite shoulders. Raise yourself off the ground until your elbows touch your thighs, then return to the ground. For minimal fitness, gradually work up to 10-20 sit-ups. Another recommended way is to lie on your back with knees bent, reach for the top of your knees, lifting your shoulder blades off the ground. Hold for 10 seconds. Repeat and gradually work up to 10-20 times. You can also do the same but roll your shoulders and push your right hand against the outside of the left knee; return and then raise your left hand against the outside of the right knee. This way helps to develop the oblique muscles on each side of the abdomen.

Weight training: This is the use of free weights such as dumbbells, barbells, and exercise machines. Exercise machines that are most used are Universal Gym and Nautilus. It is recommended that children under age 13 not use weight training but calisthenics to develop strength and endurance. The principle for weight training is that for strength you lift heavy weight a few times, whereas for endurance you lift lighter weights a greater number of times. It is important to receive proper instruction so as to learn proper safety measures and proper techniques before engaging in a weight training program. Teenagers who use weight training are encouraged to be under adult supervision. Three days a week, every other day, is the recommended frequency for weight training. (A good resource book for weight training and fitness is *Sensible Fitness* by Jack H. Wilmore, Ph.D., Leisure Press.)

Recreational and sports activities do offer exercise, but a good principle to remember is: do not play sports to get in shape, but get in shape to play sports.

Most sports have more to do with offering skill-related fitness than health-related fitness. Popular games such as baseball, basketball, football, tennis, racquetball, and golf, although they are fun, are stop and go and therefore offer less aerobic benefits than continuous and rhythmic movement that involves large muscle groups. Games that consist of quick movement and short bursts of speed are not as beneficial for cardiovascular fitness.

There is a great deal to be gained from sports and recreational activities, values that Pope Pius XII and Pope John Paul II have touched on in their teachings: values such as loyalty, friendship, respect, discipline, fair play, solidarity, and a spirit of cooperation.

The American Academy of Pediatrics recommends that children do not engage in team sports before the age of six. Some other medical experts and physical education professionals do not recommend intense athletic competition before the age of 10. They state that activities should not be used in comparing performance between children, but should emphasize learning basic skills, socialization, and just plain having fun. They recommend starting with swimming, biking, and running activities as ways of moving into team sports.

Parents should teach their children at an early age locomotor skills such as running, skipping, jumping, hopping, galloping, and balancing. Manipulative skills such as throwing, catching, kicking, dribbling, and rolling a ball should also be taught. These are all sports-related skills that can help children later on in athletic achievements, according to their developmental age and their likes. It is important that fathers and mothers exercise and play with their children and organize family games, hikes, and walks. (A good resource book for locomotor and non-locomotor skills and elementary physical education information is: *Dynamic Physical Education for Elementary School Children* by Victor P. Dauer and Robert P. Pangrazi, Burgess Publishing Co.)

INTENSITY

It is important to maintain a sufficiently high heart rate while exercising, so that you achieve a "training effect." The target heart rate is the rate at which your heart should be beating so that you achieve the maximum aerobic conditioning effect. There is a target heart rate zone that can be determined so as to help you determine what intensity you should maintain during exercise. It is determined by first calculating your maximum heart rate. There are several accepted formulas for arriving at your maximum heart rate; one is:

[220 minus your age = maximum heart rate]

You then calculate your target heart rate by using a percentage formula of your maximum heart rate. Some recommend 60 percent to 70 percent of your maximum heart rate for people who have been sedentary for some time. Others recommend 65 to 80 percent of your maximum heart rate as an overall formula. So to find your target heart rate zone, you would multiply .65 times your maximum heart rate to determine the range at which you should maintain your heart rate per minute during exercise. Let's say you are 40 years old - your maximum heart rate is 220-40 = 180. You then multiply 180 x 0.65 = 117, then 180 x 0.80 = 144. So the range in which you should exercise is 117-144. You can monitor your heart rate during exercise and immediately after exercise by taking your pulse with the tips of two fingers on the radial artery (on the inside of your wrist, below the base of your thumb), or by pressing lightly on the carteroid artery of your neck (on either side of the Adam's apple) with index and middle fingers. You then use a watch and count your pulse for 15 seconds and then multiply by 4 to arrive at your heart rate per minute. You can also use the talk test instead of taking your pulse. Basically, this is listening to your body and exercising at a rate where you can carry on a regular conversation during exercise; if you get out of breath and cannot speak in a regular fashion, you are exercising too fast. The key is to take it gradually. Know your limits and do not push yourself beyond them. Generally, adults need 8 to 10 weeks to get into fairly good shape after being sedentary. If you gradually adapt your body to regular exercise, you lessen your chances of injury and discouragement. Start off at the lower range of your target zone until you think your fitness has improved, and then gradually move on to the upper range.

FREQUENCY AND DURATION

To build cardiovascular fitness, it is recommended that you exercise 3-5 days per week. The time of exercise refers to your activity that is maintained within your target heart rate zone. This does not include warm-up and cool-down. Beginners are recommended to start off with 10-20 minutes of aerobic activity.

Those in average and good shape are recommended to do 20-30 minutes of aerobic activity. Children around ages 6-9 should limit their activity to 10-20 minutes of imaginative aerobic activity. Beginners are recommended to limit themselves to short periods of vigorous exercise, mixed with moderate levels. Many people start their time with walking. They are more likely not to get injured and stay with their program than are people who start with vigorous exercise. Remember, sore muscles are inevitable in the beginning, but this will lessen with regular exercise.

After medical clearance has been obtained and the exercise program taken into consideration, a total exercise program should include: 1) a warm-up and stretching period, 2) the aerobic conditioning period, 3) the cool-down.

The warm-up and stretching period: This is a 5 to 10 minute period used to gradually prepare your body with low-level activity for the more vigorous aerobic activity that follows. This low-level activity includes static stretching (slow tension) exercises, along with moving at a slow pace at whatever main activity you are going to do. The stretch exercises are used to improve flexibility and prepare the muscles, joints, and ligaments for the stress that follows from your main activity. The moving slowly increases your circulation and warms and stretches the muscles, preparing them for forceful contractions. It also gradually accelerates your heart rate preparing it to be maintained within the target heart rate zone during exercise. This warm-up period is very important for helping to reduce muscle and joint soreness.

Static stretch exercises are to be done easily and gently, avoiding bouncing and jerking. These exercises stretch the muscles beyond their normal length to the greatest possible length. It is best to stretch slowly until the muscles and connective tissue come to a point of tension that creates "stretch pain," a slight to moderate discomfort. You then hold the position for 10-30 seconds. Relax and then repeat the exercise 3-5 times. Avoid overstretching, as it can lead to injury. Some professionals advocate stretching after a few minutes of moving slowly, such as walking or easy jogging, stating that it is easier to stretch a warm muscle. The following stretch exercises give attention to stretching hamstring, calf, and low back muscles so as to reduce soreness and risk of injury:

Procedure: Lie on your back, bend and bring one of your knees up to your chest, hold tight for 10 seconds. Relax and repeat with other leg 3 to 5 times with each leg. Stretches low back muscles and hip flexor.

Procedure: Lie on your back, bring both knees to the chest, hold tight for 10 seconds, then straighten both legs and relax. Repeat 3-5 times. Stretches low back muscles.

Procedure: Lie on your back with your knees bent. Bring one knee toward chest, then extend the leg in a straight line upward, then lock your knee in so as to keep leg straight. Hold for 10 seconds. Relax and then repeat with the other leg. Repeat 3-5 times with each leg. Stretches the hamstring muscles (muscle behind the thigh).

Procedure: Stand facing a wall, about 3 feet away. In a lunge position, bring one foot forward while keeping the back leg straight and heel flat to the floor. Allow the knee of the front leg to bend and lean forward as far as comfortably possible. Hold for 10-30 seconds. Relax and then repeat with the other leg. Repeat 3 to 5 times with each leg. As your flexibility improves, stand further away from the wall. Stretches calf muscles. (A good resource book for more stretches and information on fitness is *Being Fit - A Personal Guide* by Bud Getchell, Ph.D., John Wiley & Sons, Inc.)

The aerobic conditioning period: This period is the "heart" of your individual and family exercise program. Remember to do activities that you enjoy, so that you will keep them up and view exercise as a lifetime activity. It is an excellent idea to do aerobic activities as a family, remembering also that everyone needs variety, especially children. The exercise prescription outlined earlier in the chapter gives the details of this period. Remember that aerobic conditioning helps you get in shape for the games and sports that you like. Remember also to drink plenty of water before, during, and after aerobic exercise, especially during hot weather.

Cool-down period: This is a period of 5-10 minutes. Just as in the warm-up period, when the body is gradually prepared for the main activity by progressive increase in activity; the cool-down period is used to gradually lower the level of the main activity. This is done by continuing your walking, cycling, swimming, jogging, but at a slower rate. This is done so as to allow your muscles to help in pumping the blood from your extremities back to your heart, especially the blood in your lower extremities. The cool-down also helps to lower body temperature and excess norepinephrine, which is present after vigorous exercise. It is also recommended to do some stretching exercises during this period, so as to prevent or reduce joint and muscle soreness. These stretches should be done following the initial slowing down period. One can also extend this period to include working on muscular strength and endurance by means of calisthenics or weight training.

NUTRITION

It is extremely important to develop a sound game plan as far as nutrition is concerned. It is necessary for establishing and maintaining a solid foundation for our bodies; one that will serve the purpose for which God created them: to be temples of the Holy Spirit. Proper nutrition provides a solid base for developing our physical, emotional, and spiritual well-being. Proper nutrition, along with exercise and rest, contributes to the development and maintenance of a vigorous, healthy body. It is well to remember that without proper nutrition, we will not have the needed energy for exercise. What you eat will determine your level of energy. It is good to think of food as human fuel; fuel that is needed for the efficient operation of our bodies. A person who eats the proper foods provides himself with the proper energy to do justice to his vocation in life and its many duties, in accordance with the will of God.

There are certain principles of nutrition that are well to be considered. Parents must be models for their children in learning and incorporating these principles into their lives. Children with poor eating habits will be affected throughout the different phases of their development.

An individual or family should eat three meals a day, meals that include a variety of foods containing carbohydrates, protein, and fat; foods that are selected from the four food groups: fruits and vegetables, bread and cereal, milk group, and meat group. It is recommended to eat food that is low in fat and sugar and high in fiber.

Carbohydrates are important because they are the main source of energy for our muscles. Carbohydrates also provide glucose, the crucial energy source for the brain. They also provide needed vitamins and minerals and are high in water content and fiber, which is needed for digestion. Complex carbohydrates are found in food such as fruits, vegetables, potatoes, pasta, corn, and whole wheat bread. It is recommended that 50 to 60 percent of your total calories be carbohydrates.

Protein is needed for repairing tissue and building up new tissue. It serves as an energy reserve when energy from carbohydrates is burned out. Food such as fish, poultry, cheese, milk, eggs, and beans are good sources of protein. It is recommended that 15 to 20 percent of your total calories be protein.

Fat is a stored source of energy that we burn during rest and light to moderate exercise. It should consist of 25 to 30 percent of your total calories.

It is important to drink six glasses of water a day. A basic principle for weight control consists of balancing the calories we take in with the energy or physical activity we put out. The extra body fat is caused not so much by taking in more calories as it is in decreasing the amount of exercise we do. (An excellent resource book for nutrition, weight control, and aerobic fitness is: *The Aerobic Program for Total Well-Being* by Kenneth Cooper, M.D., M.Ph., Bantam Books.)

10

Spiritual Fitness and Athletes of the Faith

Pope John Paul II, in his homily at a Mass on May 10, 1993 in Caltanissetta, Sicily, talked about how St. Paul compared two types of athletes: athletes of sport and athletes of the faith. The Pope encouraged the young people in attendance to represent both. St. Paul ennobled exercise and sports with his own Christian perspective. He viewed everything we do, including exercise and sports, as means of giving glory to God. He viewed the body as God's creation and encouraged us to glorify God by making our bodies the shrines of His presence - just think, shrines of the Holy Spirit.

Perhaps today, we need to question ourselves on how our physical fitness and athletic competition influence our spiritual development. Do we view physical exercise and sports as a school which develops the natural virtues that form a solid foundation for the supernatural virtues, taking into mind the principle: "grace builds on nature"? The Pope had stated: "All sports can and must be formative; that is, they can and must contribute to the integral development of the 'human person.'"[54] In his Christian Humanism, based on St. Thomas Aquinas' metaphysics of the human person, the Pope stressed the dignity of the human person who is made in the image and likeness of God. The Pope proposed a renewed vision of sport based on the principle that the dignity of the human person is the goal and criterion of all sporting activity.

St. Paul emphasizes the interior and spiritual significance

of sport. In his writings he describes the athletes in the Greek and Roman stadiums receiving a reward, a perishable wreath. He then writes about Christians receiving an imperishable reward, eternal life. St. Paul used sporting images to illustrate the life of struggle of the Christian on earth. He wrote: "You know well enough that when men run in a race, the race is for all, but the prize for one; run then; for victory" (1 Cor 9:24). And in another time, he wrote: "Fight the good fight of faith" (1 Tim 6:12).

St. Paul, drawing from the concepts of the sporting culture of Greece, wrote about the importance of discipline and temperance in attaining eternal life. He wrote: "Every athlete exercises self-control in all things" (1 Cor 9:25). St. Ignatius of Antioch in his letter to Polycarp builds on this: "Be temperate, like an athlete of God; the prize is immortality and eternal life."[55] St. Paul wrote to the Corinthians:

> Every athlete must keep all his appetites under control; and he does it to win a crown that fades, whereas ours is imperishable. So I do not run my course like a man in doubt of his goal; I do not fight my battle like a man who wastes his blows on the air. I buffet my own body, and make it my slave; or I, who have preached to others, may myself be rejected as worthless. (1 Cor 9:25-27)

Perhaps today we should also question ourselves on the amount of time we spend on our spiritual fitness compared to our physical fitness. The first place in man's composite being does not belong to the body, but to the soul. In the union of body and soul that forms our one nature, the principle element is the soul and not the body, which is the instrument of the soul. St. Thomas Aquinas said it well when he referred to exercise and sports as perfecting the body as an instrument of the mind and makes the mind a more refined instrument for the search and communication of truth. Winning victories of the soul is what we are to be about.

The early Father of the Church, Clement of Alexandria, clearly valued physical and spiritual fitness, but of the two, he taught that spiritual fitness is the most excellent; "that by it, the soul is made beautiful with the presence of the Holy Spirit and adornments He confers: justice, prudence, fortitude, temperance, love of the good, and modesty." He taught that physical exercise cultivates symmetry of body members and produces a good complexion. He also taught that physical exercise is effective in maintaining health and a pleasing physical appearance.

As far as spiritual fitness is concerned, one could suppose that if one bestowed equally serious care on the interior life, as one does on exercise and sports, one would certainly be well on the road to sanctity. On October 29, 2000 in Rome's Olympic Stadium, John Paul II prayed to Jesus and asked Him to help athletes to put the same effort into personal asceticism that they do into sports. Perhaps it is worth remembering: "Seek ye therefore first the kingdom of God and His justice and all these things shall be added until you" (Matt 6:33). The late eminent French Dominican theologian Reginald Garrigou-Lagrange, O.P. in his classic book on the spiritual life, *The Three Ages of the Interior Life*, wrote: "The interior life is for all the one thing necessary. It ought to be constantly developing in our soul; more so than what we call our intellectual life, more so than our scientific, artistic, or literary life."[56]

MODELS

All the saints can be called victorious athletes of the faith. One such saint is St. Dominic, whom the Church has designated a "holy athlete of Christ." It was Pope Innocent III who called him "the invincible athlete of Christ." Pope Honorius called the members of his Order, the Dominican Order, "champions of the faith and the true lights of the world" and the "invincible athletes of Christ." Dante called him "the athlete of Christ." St. Dominic was a man of indefatigable energy, a man of great character and depth. Joyousness sprang out of the great physical energy and immense strength of bodily endurance that he possessed. He was truly an athlete of the faith, capable of doing great things.

St. Dominic was pre-eminently a man of prayer. It was the source of his inner power and tranquility of his exterior graciousness. He was trained to look upon success as achieved not by his convincing eloquence or the logic of his argument, but by a supernatural weapon, the power of prayer. The Divine Office and the Rosary were his favorite prayers. He prayed before the Blessed Sacrament as often as he could. St. Dominic used his body in his manner of addressing God in prayer: bowing, kneeling, standing, prostrating himself, using every posture and gesture of the body. His idea of using his body in prayer was due to the rendering to God of the whole of man; every gift, or faculty, or soul, or body. He was very devoted to the Mass. The New Testament was his favorite study and made the textbook of life. He constantly carried the Gospel of St. Matthew and the Epistles of St. Paul with him.

Tradition affirms that Mary herself revealed to him the Rosary in the form of mental and vocal prayer. He prayed the Rosary by contemplating on the character and virtues of Our Lord, on His mysteries - joined by saying the Our Father and Hail Marys, which were noted by a string of beads. His method of preaching was to mention and develop a certain mystery of the faith, and then pray the Our Father and Hail Mary divided into decades. The mysteries that were chosen at that time were chosen to combat definite error. St. Dominic used the Rosary for correcting the false dogmas of the Albigensians, who had an unnatural hatred of life. As the mysteries of the faith were gradually brought back to the minds and hearts of the people, mysteries of falsehood disappeared. The doctrine of the Incarnation, so specially commemorated in the Rosary, became, then, as ever, the bulwark of the truth. St. Dominic loved praying the Rosary day and night. He knew the human heart and it is the adaptation of the Rosary to the needs of the heart that gave this form of prayer its freshness and popularity. His Rosary was his preparation for every sermon. His most famous spiritual son, St. Thomas Aquinas, would one day say: "It is better to illumine than merely to shine."

Another athlete of the faith recognized by the Church is Blessed Pier Giorgio Frassati. He was beatified by Pope John Paul II on May 20, 1990. The Pope spoke of him as being a model for athletes on April 12, 1984.

Pier was open to the values of sports. He was an avid mountain climber who valued it as a means of developing character. He admired, in the pure atmosphere of the mountains, the magnificence of God. In this pristine environment of the mountains, he found it easy to contemplate, seeing God reflected in His creation. This led him to lift up his mind and heart to God in a spirit of prayer, offering praise and gratitude to God. He was also an able skier, never missing making a visit to the Blessed Sacrament after skiing. He was very devoted to the Mass, attending it and receiving Communion every day. He had a practice of making frequent visits to the Blessed Sacrament.

He was also very fond of swimming, rowing, and bicycle riding. He was a man of deep prayer who recognized the chief ends of prayer: adoration, reparation, thanksgiving, and petition. He loved praying the Rosary. He prayed the Rosary three times a day after he became a member of the Third Order of St. Dominic. He treasured the Rosary, which, in a sense, epitomizes Dominican spirituality; offering a way of meditating, pondering, and proclaiming the truths of faith expressed in the form of praise.

His infectious smile and joy of living attracted followers. He was born to give and not just to live for himself. He loved the poor; he passed through their midst doing good to them. His fondness for the epistles of St. Paul sparked his zeal for fraternal charity.

Pier was interested in the social teachings of the Catholic Church. He gave time and money to help establish a Catholic daily newspaper, *Momento*, which was based on the principles of the papal social encyclical *Rerum Novarum*. He desired that the social teachings of the Catholic Church would influence the culture of his time.

Polio struck Blessed Pier at the age of 24. He had no fear of death, saying, "I think the day of my death will be the happiest day of my life." He died with a smile on his face and a Rosary in his hand.

PRESCRIPTION FOR SPIRITUAL FITNESS

Athletes and coaches are familiar with having a game plan for their upcoming contest. They know what it takes to prepare themselves for putting forth their best effort in order to win. The game plan involves using the best strategy, using the best plays from the playbook that will produce the advantage, the winning edge.

Those who pursue spiritual fitness, athletes of the faith, are like athletes of the field: loyal to the training rules and training aids, not allowing tiredness nor any obstacle to halt them until their goal is reached, eternal life with God. They are aware that they need to train, to develop a spirituality so that they can be builders of the civilization of love here on earth and to save their soul and be united with God in heaven for eternity. They know that the self-discipline developed through physical fitness and sports will help them develop a proper mindset, a proper attitude in striving for eternal life with God. Athletes of the faith recognize the need for a game plan that includes self-denial and self-mastery in the moral life, so as to gain the imperishable reward. They know that the Christian life demands systematic spiritual training, since the Christian "like every athlete exercises self-control in all things" (1 Cor 9:25).

Athletes of the faith are like athletes of sport who display persistence in resisting exhaustion, knowing that they must develop the perseverance of a marathon runner, knowing that Jesus said: "By patient endurance you will save your lives" (Luke 21:19). These athletes of the faith know that the spiritual life demands patience, not expecting it to be easy; for them physical fitness and sports have tempered the character and have formed a will as hard as steel so that they can say with St. Paul: "I buffet my body and make it my slave" (1 Cor 9:27), and so practice mortification and with God's grace, practice the virtues.

Athletes of sport look to their instructors, their coaches, for supplying them with a game plan, a strategy, a set of plays from the playbook that will give them an advantage, that will put them into a position to be victorious. With their eyes set on victory, they submit to the instruction and discipline of the coach.

Athletes of the faith look to the Catholic Church and to the Vicar of Christ for their instruction, for their game plan; a strategy that will put them into a position to be victorious in gaining eternal life with God. God, who wants all men to be saved and to know the truth (1 Tim 2:4), has given mankind the Catholic Church to teach man the light of the truth, which leads to eternal life. God has entrusted to the Catholic Church the correct interpretation of the divinely revealed truth on man's redemption and his inheritance of eternal life. In Karol Wojtyla's (Pope John Paul II) book, The Way to Christ, he mentions that:

> The Church was organized from within by Christ himself, who said to Peter: 'You are Peter, and on this rock I will build my church, and the powers of death shall not prevail against it. I will give you the keys of the kingdom of heaven, and whatever you bind on earth, shall be bound in heaven, and whatever you loose on earth, shall be loosed in heaven (Matt 16:16-18).[57]

In these words, we see Peter and every successor of his to be the rock on which the Catholic Church is built, the one who is to be strong and faithful, the one to give stability to Christ's Church.

Benedict XVI, the new successor of Peter, is the rock on which the Church of our time is built. Benedict XVI was a bike rider as a youth and has been a walker in his adult life. On June 5, 2005 Benedict XVI talked about how sport, health, and nature are linked and how he hoped that sport practiced in a healthy and harmonious way at all levels will encourage brotherhood and solidarity between people. The athlete of the faith looks to the Catholic Church and Benedict XVI as their instructors. For the athlete of the faith to cross the finish line and be victorious in receiving the imperishable prize that God offers, they need to submit to the teachings of the Catholic Church and Benedict XVI, just as the athlete of sport needs to submit to the instructions of the coach in order to carry off a victory. There are three highly recommended books written by Cardinal Joseph Ratzinger, now Benedict XVI. They are an autobiography called *Milestones* and two interview-format books called *Salt of the Earth* and *God and the World*. He has written many other books besides these before becoming Pope.

Ojciec Święty Benedykt XVI

The athlete of the faith needs to submit to the teachings of Benedict XVI, as the athlete of sport needs to submit to the instructions of the coach in order to carry off a victory.

TRAINING AIDS

The competition today for the athlete of the faith is secular humanism; a viewpoint that sees nature as self-sufficient and human life as the only life there is. It denies the existence of God, His revelation, supernatural life, and eternal life with God. In order for the athlete of the faith to be spiritually strong against this foe, he must make use of the training aids the Church offers. They are: 1) instruction for the renewal of the mind, 2) prayer, and 3) the sacraments.

INSTRUCTION FOR THE RENEWAL OF THE MIND

St. Paul in his letter to the Romans stated: "Do not be conformed to this world, but be transformed by the renewal of your mind" (Rom 12:2). The Church offers the Sacred Scriptures, especially the Gospels, in helping us renew our minds. The Second Vatican Council refers to the Gospels as "the source of all saving truth and moral teaching" (*Dei Verbum*, n.7). The Church also offers her athletes of the faith the *Catechism of the Catholic Church*, the newest compendium of Catholic doctrine; a statement of the Church's faith and of Catholic doctrine. The Catechism is intended for all the faithful who wish to deepen their knowledge of the unfathomable riches of salvation. The Catechism is offered to all who want to know what the Catholic Church believes. John Paul II said: "It is a gift which the Heavenly Father grants to His children offering them through this Catechism the possibility of knowing Him better in the light of the spirit." *The Compendium of the Catechism of the Catholic Church*, presented on June 28, 2005 by Benedict XVI, is highly recommended.

Athletes of the faith also have the opportunity of renewing their minds by reading the encyclical letters and apostolic exhortations of Pope John Paul II. The Pope's Encyclical Letter *The Splendor of Truth* is a marvelous work which is meant to be a companion to the *Catechism of the Catholic Church*. It is a splendid reflection on the principles of the moral life. It reaffirms the dignity and greatness of the human person, created in God's image; it sets forth the concept of freedom and how it is related to Jesus' words: "The Truth will make you free." The social teachings of the Church that are contained in John Paul's encyclicals are indispensable for the athlete of the faith in understanding the social, economic, political, and cultural aspects of his or her life.

The guiding principle of the Church's social teaching is the correct view of the human person and his or her unique value, being created in the image and likeness of God. Three of John Paul's encyclicals that deal with the social teachings of the Church are: *On Human Work, On Social Concern*, and *On the Hundredth Anniversary of Rerum Novarum*. An excellent work of John Paul's that deals with the true nature of man is his first Encyclical Letter, *The Redeemer of Man*.

The Church also offers her athletes of the faith a proper understanding and vision of marriage, human sexuality, and family life. Pope Paul VI's Encyclical Letter *Humantae Vitae* represents a call to reverence God's vision of marriage and human sexuality. John Paul's Apostolic Exhortation *The Role of the Christian Family in the Modern World* is also an excellent work for the proper understanding of God's plan for marriage and the family. Excellent companions to this work would be John Paul's Apostolic Exhortation *Guardian of the Redeemer,* a work on St. Joseph, and his Apostolic Letter *On the Dignity and Vocation of Woman*. Four highly recommended books written by John Paul II are *Crossing the Threshold of Hope*, his 1996 memoirs *Gift and Mystery*, the second to his last book, *Rise, Let Us Be On Our Way*, and his final book, *Memory and Identity: Conversations Between Millenniums*. The apostolic letter John Paul II wrote on the Rosary, called *The Rosary of the Virgin Mary*, published in 2002 (see appendix), is highly recommended for athletes of the faith to help them be devoted to Mary and her holy Rosary. The encyclical letter that John Paul II wrote on the Eucharist called *Ecclesia de Eucharistia* is also highly recommended to help athletes of the faith to love and have a great devotion to the Eucharist.

PRAYER

The athlete of sport uses exercise and nutrition to build up strength for the game on the field. The athlete of the faith uses prayer to build up spiritual strength for the game of life and for achieving the final reward of eternal life with God. Prayer is the simplest and most widely practiced way of obtaining grace; grace needed to lead to victory over sin and its forces, grace to keep us close to God and to inwardly transform us, grace needed to strengthen the work of conscience in directing us to the true and good.

St. John Damascene defines prayer as "the lifting up of the mind and heart to God." St. Augustine wrote that to love and possess God in the everlasting security of eternal life should be the final object of all our prayers. St. Thomas Aquinas, universal teacher of the Church, reminds us that prayer should be made with confidence, rectitude, order, devoutness, and humility. Through his teachings we learn that prayer benefits us in three ways; it remedies evil, it obtains that which we desire, and it establishes friendship with God. (An excellent book on prayer written by St. Thomas Aquinas is *The Three Greatest Prayers*, Sophia Press.)

Prayer is truly a gift from God. St. Francis de Sales, in his classic, *The Introduction to the Devout Life*, states:

> Prayer places our intellect in the brilliance of God's light and exposes our will to the warmth of his heavenly love; nothing else so effectively purifies our intellect of ignorance and our will of depraved affections.[58]

As far as mental prayer is concerned, this great saint, a true instructor in spiritual skills, advises us that the life and death of Jesus is the most fitting and profitable subject that can be chosen for our ordinary meditations. He advises that vocal prayer, such as the Our Father or Hail Mary, be said with feeling and not quickly or hurriedly. Vocal and mental prayer includes acts of adoration, thanksgiving, petition, and reparation. The prayer of petition acknowledges the truth that God alone is the source of all good things.

We remember on television the Nike commercial with the words: "Life is short - play hard." Would not the saying "Life is short - pray hard" be more fitting for the athlete of the faith? We also see football teams on television using the desperation pass called the "Hail Mary pass" for a last-resort, seconds-to-go play; whereas the athlete of the faith hears the Church teach us to pray continually and not just in times of urgent need or emergency.

Though we are called to private prayer, we are also called to prayer with others. Jesus said: "Again I say to you - if two of you agree on earth about anything they ask, it will be done for them by my Father in heaven. For when two or three are gathered in my name, there am I in the midst of them." Pope John Paul II urged family prayer, especially the family Rosary. In his Apostolic Exhortation *The Role of the Christian Family in the Modern World*, he stated:

> Only by praying together with their children can a father and mother penetrate the inner-most depths of their children's hearts and leave an impression that the future events in their lives will not be able to efface.[59]

John Paul II, a man of deep prayer, saw work as taking up most of our time. But he believed that all activities should be rooted in prayer, as though in a spiritual soil, and that the depth of this soil must not be too thin. He saw his own thoughts and words pass through prayer, conforming to the Thomistic principle - hand on to others the fruits of your prayer.

It is very beneficial and fitting for the athlete of the faith to pray to the Holy Spirit for enlightenment and guidance and to seek His help in knowing what to pray for. In his first Encyclical Letter *The Redeemer of Man*, John Paul II referred to the prayer:

> Come, Holy Spirit! Come! Come! Heal our wounds, our strength renew; On our dryness pour your dew; Wash the stains of guilt away; Bend the stubborn heart and will; Melt the frozen, warm the chill; Guide the steps that go astray.[60]

218 THE CATHOLIC IDEAL: EXERCISE AND SPORTS

He referred to this appeal to the Holy Spirit as being a means of obtaining the Holy Spirit and also as an answer to the "materialisms" of our age. In his Encyclical Letter *The Splendor of Truth*, the Pope wrote:

> The Spirit of Jesus, received by the humble and docile heart of the believer, brings about the flourishing of Christian moral life and the witness of holiness amid the great variety of vocations, gifts, responsibilities, conditions, and life situations.[61]

An excellent work which helps in developing a better knowledge of and devotion to the Holy Spirit is John Paul's Encyclical Letter *On the Holy Spirit in the Life of the Church and the World*.

The Rosary is the most popular devotional prayer. Many popes have praised the Rosary as a spiritual training school where people whose muscles of the spirit have grown flabby and atrophied can slowly and normally win back the strength required to come off victoriously in the great battle of life. Pope Paul VI, in his Apostolic Exhortation *For the Right Ordering and Development of Devotion to the Blessed Virgin Mary*, devoted a section of it to the Rosary. He described the Rosary as "the compendium of the entire Gospel."

The Rosary has all the necessary ingredients of prayer. John Paul II taught that:

> The Rosary is a prayer 'concerning Mary' united with Christ in His salvific mission. At the same time it is a prayer 'to Mary'...our best mediatrix with her Son. Finally, it is a prayer that in a special way we recite 'with Mary' as the Apostles in the Upper Room prayed with her, preparing themselves to receive the Holy Spirit.[62]

John Paul II wrote a marvelous encyclical letter on Mary called *Mother of the Redeemer*, which is highly recommended for the athlete of the faith who wishes to develop a filial relationship with

Mary, his spiritual mother.

Mary is the most perfect model of Christian contemplation. Praying the Rosary with Mary, she will enlighten our minds and teach us the meaning of each of the 20 mysteries. The athlete of the faith will then pray like Mary did, when he ponders over the mysteries that Mary pondered during her life on earth and which she continues to do in heaven. Mary appeared at Fatima, Portugal in 1917 and asked that the Rosary be prayed every day. She has promised many graces and blessings for those who pray the Rosary. John Cassian, a spiritual writer in the fourth century, wrote of the athlete of the faith partaking in an Olympic struggle against vices. One of Mary's promises to those who pray the Rosary is that it will destroy vice and decrease sin.

In his apostolic letter on the Rosary (see appendix) that he wrote during the Year of the Rosary in 2002, John Paul II wrote:

> The Rosary is a prayer loved by countless Saints and encouraged by the Magisterium. It is destined to bring forth a harvest of holiness. What is needed is a Christian life distinguished above all in the art of prayer. The Rosary is an effective spiritual weapon against the evils afflicting society. With the Rosary, the Christian people sits at the school of Mary and is led to contemplate the beauty on the face of Christ and to experience the depths of his love. Through the Rosary the faithful receive abundant grace, as though from the very hands of the Mother of the Redeemer.[63]

The young athlete of the faith is to be encouraged to pray the Rosary every day by the very words of John Paul II in his apostolic letter on the Rosary:

> There is nothing to stop children and young people from praying it with practical aids to understanding and appreciation. If the Rosary is well presented, I am sure that young people will once more make this prayer their own and recite it with the enthusiasm typical of their age group.[64]

It would be helpful for the athlete of the faith to know that Mary will be very pleased with you after you pray the Rosary properly, as she was with young St. Bernadette at Lourdes, France in 1858. When Bernadette finished praying the Rosary, Mary would smile at her. According to St. Bernadette, it seemed all Mary did was smile. A very good book that will help athletes of the faith find the practical aids, understanding, and appreciation of the Rosary the Pope talked about in his apostolic letter is *The Rosary: The Little Summa* (Aquinas Press).

THE SACRAMENTS

Another power-source for the athlete of the faith is the sacraments. Jesus established in the Catholic Church the seven sacraments in order to give to those who receive them a share in the grace which He won for each person through His passion, death, and resurrection. The Second Vatican Council referred to the purpose of the sacraments as being: to sanctify men, to build up the Body of Christ and give worship to God.

The athlete of the faith has the opportunity to receive the sacraments of the Eucharist and Penance frequently. The Church encourages her members to unite themselves more closely to Christ through these sacraments. St. Thomas Aquinas wrote of these two sacraments in terms of the life of the spirit having a certain similarity to the life of the body.

THE EUCHARIST

In the life of the body, man requires food so that his life may be preserved and sustained; so also in the life of the spirit, after being fortified, he requires spiritual food, which is Christ's body: "Unless you shall eat of the flesh of the Son of Man, and drink of His blood, you shall not have life in you" (John 6:54). The Second Vatican Council described the Mass as "the primary and indispensable source from which the faithful are to derive the true Christian spirit" (Constitution on the Sacred Liturgy, n. 4). It also taught that "the Eucharist is the source and summit of

Christian life" (n. 4).

John Paul II, in his encyclical letter on the Eucharist, stated:

> For the holy Eucharist contains the Church's entire spiritual wealth: Christ himself, our Passover and living bread. Through his own flesh, now made living and life-giving by the Holy Spirit, he offers life to men. Consequently the gaze of the Church is constantly turned to her Lord, present in the Sacrament of the Altar, in which she discovers the full manifestation of his boundless love.[65]

John Paul II stated that the Eucharist "stands at the center of the Church's life" and that the Church draws her life, her nourishment, from it. The athlete of the faith is encouraged to receive the Eucharist as often as possible.

The athlete of the faith is also encouraged to make frequent visits to the Blessed Sacrament. Christ in his glorified body, with his face shining like the sun, in all the tabernacles of the world, lovingly waits for us to come to him, so as to smile on us and shed his light on us. John Paul II stated in his encyclical letter on the Eucharist:

> The worship of the Eucharist outside of the Mass is of inestimable value for the life of the Church. It is pleasant to spend time with him, to lie close to his breast like the Beloved Disciple and to feel the infinite love present in his heart. This practice, repeatedly praised and recommended by the Magisterium, is supported by the example of many saints. St. Alphonsus Liguori wrote: 'Of all devotions, that of adoring Jesus in the Blessed Sacrament is the greatest after the sacraments, the one dearest to God and the one most helpful to us.' [66]

PENANCE

In the life of the body, a man is sometimes sick, and unless he takes medicine, he will die. Likewise, in the life of the spirit, a man is sick on account of sin; thus, he needs medicine that he may be restored to health. This grace is bestowed in the Sacrament of Penance. The Church recommends frequent confession for advancement in the path of virtue, for true knowledge of ourselves, for bad habits to be uprooted, for our conscience to be purified and our will strengthened. It is highly recommended for the athlete of the faith to consider going to confession at least once a month. Pope John Paul II wrote an excellent apostolic exhortation on Penance called *On Reconciliation and Penance.*

In conclusion, the two main power sources for the athlete of the faith are prayer and the sacraments. The sacraments, meritorious good works, and prayer are powerful means of obtaining the grace necessary for the athlete of the faith to receive the crown; the imperishable reward of union and possession of God in heaven.

About the Author

Robert Feeney grew up in Alexandria, Virginia. He holds a Bachelor of Arts degree in Physical Education from Carroll College in Helena, Montana, and a Master of Science degree in P.E. from the University of Dayton. He has enjoyed physical movement and games from an early age, even before the above picture was taken. He has taught physical education and health at the grade school, high school, and university levels. He also has experience as an athletic director, coach, and high school religion teacher, in addition to working in individual and corporate fitness programs and in a university human performance laboratory. He is a Vietnam war veteran who was awarded the Purple Heart and attributes being saved from near death there to Mary, the Mother of God. Cardinal Patrick O'Boyle presented him in Washington, D.C. with a plaque, "Apostle of Mary," on April 28, 1973. He is a member of the Third Order of St. Dominic and the author of the book *The Rosary: The Little Summa.*

Appendix

Apostolic Letter of John Paul II
on the Rosary

INTRODUCTION

1. The Rosary of the Virgin Mary, which gradually took form in the second millennium under the guidance of the Spirit of God, is a prayer loved by countless saints and encouraged by the Magisterium. Simple yet profound, it still remains at the dawn of this third millennium a prayer of great significance, destined to bring forth a harvest of holiness. It blends easily into the spiritual journey of the Christian life, which, after two thousand years, has lost none of the freshness of its beginnings and feels drawn by the Spirit of God to "set out into the deep" (*duc in altum!*) in order once more to proclaim and even cry out before the world that Jesus Christ is Lord and Savior, "the way, and the truth and the life" (Jn 14:6), "the goal of human history and the point on which the desires of history and civilization turn."[1]

The Rosary, though clearly Marian in character, is at heart a Christocentric prayer. In the sobriety of its elements, it has all the *depth of the Gospel message in its entirety*, of which it can be said to be a compendium.[2] It is an echo of the prayer of Mary, her

---

[1] Pastoral Constitution on the Church in the Modern World *Gaudium et Spes,* 45.

[2] Pope Paul VI, Apostolic Exhortation *Marialis Cultus* (2 February 1974), 42: AAS 66 (1974), 153.

perennial *Magnificat* for the work of the redemptive Incarnation which began in her virginal womb. With the Rosary, the Christian people *sits at the school of Mary* and is led to contemplate the beauty on the face of Christ and to experience the depths of his love. Through the Rosary the faithful receive abundant grace, as though from the very hands of the Mother of the Redeemer.

The Popes and the Rosary

2. Numerous predecessors of mine attributed great importance to this prayer. Worthy of special note in this regard is Pope Leo XIII, who on September 1, 1883 promulgated the Encyclical *Supremi Apostolatus Officio*,[3] a document of great worth, the first of his many statements about this prayer, in which he proposed the Rosary as an effective spiritual weapon against the evils afflicting society. Among the more recent Popes who from the time of the Second Vatican Council have distinguished themselves in promoting the Rosary, I would mention Blessed John XXIII[4] and above all Pope Paul VI, who in his Apostolic Exhortation *Marialis Cultus* emphasized, in the spirit of the Second Vatican Council, the Rosary's evangelical character and its Christocentric inspiration. I myself have often encouraged the frequent recitation of the Rosary. From my youthful years this prayer has held an important place in my spiritual life. I was powerfully reminded of this during my recent visit to Poland, and in particular at the Shrine of Kalwaria. The Rosary has accompanied me in moments of joy and in moments of difficulty. To it I have entrusted any number of concerns; in it I have always found comfort. Twenty-four years ago, on October 29, 1978, scarcely two weeks after my election to the See of Peter, I frankly admitted: "The Rosary is my favorite prayer. A marvelous prayer! Marvelous in its simplicity and its depth. . . It can be said that the Rosary is, in some sense, a prayer-

[3] Cf. *Acta Leonis XIII*, 3 (1884), 280-289.
[4] Particularly worthy of note is his Apostolic Epistle on the Rosary *Il religioso convegno* (29 September 1961): AAS 53 (1961), 641-647.

commentary on the final chapter of the Vatican II Constitution *Lumen Gentium*, a chapter which discusses the wondrous presence of the Mother of God in the mystery of Christ and the Church. Against the background of the words *Ave Maria*, the principal events of the life of Christ pass before the eyes of the soul. They take shape in the complete series of the joyful, sorrowful, and glorious mysteries, and they put us in living communion with Jesus through - we might say - the heart of his Mother. At the same time our heart can embrace in the decades of the Rosary all the events that make up the lives of individuals, families, nations, the Church, and all mankind - our personal concerns and those of our neighbor, especially those who are closest to us, who are dearest to us. Thus the simple prayer of the Rosary marks the rhythm of human life."[5]

With these words, dear brothers and sisters, I set *the first year of my Pontificate* within the daily rhythm of the Rosary. Today, *as I begin the twenty-fifth year of my service as the Successor of Peter*, I wish to do the same. How many graces have I received in these years from the Blessed Virgin through the Rosary: *Magnificat anima mea Dominum*! I wish to lift up my thanks to the Lord in the words of his Most Holy Mother, under whose protection I have placed my Petrine ministry: *Totus Tuus*!

October 2002 - October 2003: The Year of the Rosary

3. Therefore, in continuity with my reflection in the Apostolic Letter Novo Millennoi Ineunte, in which, after the experience of the Jubilee, I invited the People of God to "start afresh from Christ,"[6] I have felt drawn to offer a reflection on the Rosary, as a kind of Marian complement to that letter and an exhortation *to contemplate the face of Christ* in union with, and at the school of, his Most Holy Mother. To recite the Rosary is nothing other than to contemplate with Mary the face of Christ. As a way of highlighting this invitation, prompted by the forthcoming

---

[5]Angelus: Insegnamenti di Giovanni Paolo II, I (1978): 75-76.
[6]AAS 93 (2001), 285.

120th anniversary of the aforementioned encyclical of Leo XIII,
I desire that during the course of this year the Rosary should
be especially emphasized and promoted in the various Christian
communities. I therefore proclaim the year from October 2002 to
October 2003 *the Year of the Rosary.*

I leave this pastoral proposal to the initiative of each
ecclesial community. It is not my intention to encumber but rather
to complete and consolidate pastoral programs of the particular
Churches. I am confident that the proposal will find a ready and
generous reception. The Rosary, reclaimed in its full meaning,
goes to the very heart of Christian life; it offers a familiar yet
fruitful spiritual and educational opportunity for personal contemplation, the formation of the People of God, and the new evan-
gelization. I am pleased to reaffirm this also in the joyful remembrance of another anniversary: the fortieth anniversary of the
opening of the Second Vatican Ecumenical Council on October
11, 1962, the "great grace" disposed by the Spirit of God for the
Church in our time.[7]

Objections to the Rosary

4. The timeliness of this proposal is evident from a number
of considerations. First, the urgent need to counter a certain crisis
of the Rosary, which in the present historical and theological
context can risk being wrongly devalued, and therefore no longer
taught to the younger generation. There are some who think that
the centrality of the liturgy, rightly stressed by the Second Vatican
Ecumenical Council, necessarily entails giving lesser importance
to the Rosary. Yet, as Pope Paul VI made clear, not only does
this prayer not conflict with the liturgy, it also sustains it, since
it serves as an excellent introduction and a faithful echo of the
liturgy, enabling people to participate fully and interiorly in it and
to reap its fruits in their daily lives.

---

[7]During the years of preparation for the Council, Pope John XXIII
did not fail to encourage the Christian community to recite the Rosary for the
success of this ecclesial event: cf. Letter to the Cardinal Vicar (28 September
1960): AAS 52 (1960), 814-816.

Perhaps, too, there are some who fear that the Rosary is somehow unecumenical because of its distinctly Marian character. Yet the Rosary clearly belongs to the kind of veneration of the Mother of God described by the Council: a devotion directed to the Christological center of the Christian faith, in such a way that "when the Mother is honored, the Son. . . is duly known, loved, and glorified."[8] If properly revitalized, the Rosary is an aid and certainly not a hindrance to ecumenism!

A path of contemplation

5. But the most important reason for strongly encouraging the practice of the Rosary is that it represents a most effective means of fostering among the faithful that *commitment to the contemplation of the Christian mystery* which I have proposed in the Apostolic Letter *Novo Millennio Ineunte*, as a genuine "training in holiness": "What is needed is a Christian life distinguished above all in the *art of prayer*."[9] In as much as contemporary culture, even amid so many indications to the contrary, has witnessed the flowering of a new call for spirituality, due also to the influence of other religions, it is more urgent than ever that our Christian communities should become "genuine schools of prayer."[10]

The Rosary belongs among the finest and most praiseworthy traditions of Christian contemplation. Developed in the West, it is a typically meditative prayer, corresponding in some way to the "prayer of the heart" or "Jesus prayer" which took root in the soil of the Christian East.

Prayer for peace and for the family

6. A number of historical circumstances also make a revival of the Rosary quite timely. First of all, the need to implore

---

[8]Dogmatic Constitution on the Church *Lumen Gentium*, 66.
[9]No. 32: AAS 93 (2001), 288.
[10]Ibid., 33: loc. cit., 289.

from God *the gift of peace*. The Rosary has many times been proposed by my predecessors and myself as a prayer for peace. At the start of a millennium which began with the terrifying attacks of September 11, 2001, a millennium which witnesses every day in numerous parts of the world fresh scenes of bloodshed and violence, to rediscover the Rosary means to immerse oneself in contemplation of the mystery of Christ who "is our peace," since he made "the two of us one, and broke down the dividing wall of hostility" (Eph 2:14). Consequently, one cannot recite the Rosary without feeling caught up in a clear commitment to advancing peace, especially in the land of Jesus, still so sorely afflicted and so close to the heart of every Christian.

A similar need for commitment and prayer arises in relation to another critical contemporary issue: *the family*, the primary cell of society, increasingly menaced by forces of disintegration on both the ideological and practical planes, so as to make us fear for the future of this fundamental and indispensable institution and, with it, for the future of society as a whole. The revival of the Rosary in Christian families, within the context of a broader pastoral ministry to the family, will be an effective aid to countering the devastating effects of this crisis typical of our age.

"Behold, your Mother!" (Jn 19:27)

7. Many signs indicate that still today the Blessed Virgin desires to exercise through this same prayer that maternal concern to which the dying Redeemer entrusted, in the person of the beloved disciple, all the sons and daughters of the Church: "Woman, behold your son!" (Jn 19:26). Well-known are the occasions in the nineteenth and twentieth centuries on which the Mother of Christ made her presence felt and her voice heard, in order to exhort the People of God to this form of contemplative prayer. I would mention in particular, on account of their great influence on the lives of Christians and the authoritative recognition they have received from the Church, the apparitions of

---

[11]It is well-known and bears repeating that private revelations are not the same as public revelation, which is binding on the whole Church. It is the

Lourdes and of Fatima;[11] these shrines continue to be visited by great numbers of pilgrims seeking comfort and hope.

Following the witnesses

8. It would be impossible to name all the many saints who discovered in the Rosary a genuine path to growth in holiness. We need but mention Saint Louis Marie Grignion de Montfort, the author of an excellent work on the Rosary,[12] and, closer to ourselves, Padre Pio of Pietrelcina, whom I recently had the joy of canonizing. As a true apostle of the Rosary, Blessed Bartolo Longo had a special charism. His path to holiness rested on an inspiration heard in the depths of his heart: "Whoever spreads the Rosary is saved!"[13] As a result, he felt called to build a church dedicated to Our Lady of the Holy Rosary in Pompei, against the background of the ruins of the ancient city, which scarcely heard the proclamation of Christ before being buried in 79 A.D. during an eruption of Mount Vesuvius, only to emerge centuries later from its ashes as a witness to the lights and shadows of classical civilization. By his whole life's work and especially by the practice of the "Fifteen Saturdays" Bartolo Longo promoted the Christocentric and contemplative heart of the Rosary, and received great encouragement and support from Leo XIII, the "Pope of the Rosary."

task of the Magisterium to discern and recognize the authenticity and value of private revelations for the piety of the faithful.

[12] *The Secret of the Rosary.*

[13] Blessed Bartolo Longo, *Storia del Santuario di Pompei*, Pompei, 1990, 59.

CHAPTER I

CONTEMPLATING CHRIST WITH MARY

A face radiant as the sun

9. "And he was transfigured before them, and his face shone like the sun" (Mt 17:2). The Gospel scene of Christ's transfiguration, in which the three Apostles Peter, James and John appear entranced by the beauty of the Redeemer, can be seen as *an icon of Christian contemplation*. To look upon the face of Christ, to recognize its mystery amid the daily events and the sufferings of his human life, and then to grasp the divine splendour definitively revealed in the Risen Lord, seated in glory at the right hand of the Father: this is the task of every follower of Christ and therefore the task of each one of us. In contemplating Christ's face we become open to receiving the mystery of Trinitarian life, experiencing ever anew the love of the Father and delighting in the joy of the Holy Spirit. Saint Paul's words can then be applied to us: "Beholding the glory of the Lord, we are being changed into his likeness, from one degree of glory to another; for this comes from the Lord who is the Spirit" (2 Cor 3:18).

Mary, model of contemplation

10. The contemplation of Christ has an *incomparable model* in Mary. In a unique way the face of the Son belongs to Mary. It was in her womb that Christ was formed, receiving from her a human resemblance which points to an even greater spiritual closeness. No one has ever devoted himself to the contemplation of the face of Christ as faithfully as Mary. The eyes of her heart already turned to him at the Annunciation, when she conceived him by the power of the Holy Spirit. In the months that followed she began to sense his presence and to picture his features. When at last she gave birth to him in Bethlehem, her eyes were able to gaze tenderly on the face of her Son, as she "wrapped him in swaddling cloths, and laid him in a manger" (Lk2:7).

Thereafter Mary's gaze, ever filled with adoration and wonder, would never leave him. At times it would be *a questioning look*, as in the episode of the finding in the Temple: "Son, why have you treated us so?" (Lk 2:48); it would always be *a penetrating gaze,* one capable of deeply understanding Jesus, even to the point of perceiving his hidden feelings and anticipating his decisions, as at Cana (cf. Jn 2:5). At other times it would be *a look of sorrow*, especially beneath the Cross, where her vision would still be that of a mother giving birth, for Mary not only shared the passion and death of her Son, she also received the new son given to her in the beloved disciple (cf. Jn 19:26-27). On the morning of Easter hers would be *a gaze radiant with the joy of the Resurrection*, and finally, on the day of Pentecost, *a gaze afire* with the outpouring of the Spirit (cf. Acts 1:14).

Mary's memories

11. Mary lived with her eyes fixed on Christ, treasuring his every word: "She kept all these things, pondering them in her heart" (Lk 2:19; cf. 2:51). The memories of Jesus, impressed upon her heart, were always with her, leading her to reflect on the various moments of her life at her Son's side. In a way those memories were to be the "rosary" which she recited uninterruptedly throughout her earthly life.

Even now, amid the joyful songs of the heavenly Jerusalem, the reasons for her thanksgiving and praise remain unchanged. They inspire her maternal concern for the pilgrim Church, in which she continues to relate her personal account of the Gospel. *Mary constantly sets before the faithful the "mysteries" of her Son*, with the desire that the contemplation of those mysteries will release all their saving power. In the recitation of the Rosary, the Christian community enters into contact with the memories and the contemplative gaze of Mary.

The Rosary, a contemplative prayer

12. The Rosary, precisely because it starts with Mary's

own experience, is *an exquisitely contemplative prayer*. Without this contemplative dimension, it would lose its meaning, as Pope Paul VI clearly pointed out: "Without contemplation, the Rosary is a body without a soul, and its recitation runs the risk of becoming a mechanical repetition of formulas, in violation of the admonition of Christ: 'In praying do not heap up empty phrases as the Gentiles do; for they think they will be heard for their many words' (Mt 6:7). By its nature the recitation of the Rosary calls for a quiet rhythm and a lingering pace, helping the individual to meditate on the mysteries of the Lord's life as seen through the eyes of her who was closest to the Lord. In this way the unfathomable riches of these mysteries are disclosed"[14]

It is worth pausing to consider this profound insight of Paul VI, in order to bring out certain aspects of the Rosary which show that it is really a form of Christocentric contemplation.

Remembering Christ with Mary

13. Mary's contemplation is above all *a remembering*. We need to understand this word in the biblical sense of remembrance (*zakar*) as a making present of the works brought about by God in the history of salvation. The Bible is an account of saving events culminating in Christ himself. These events not only belong to "yesterday"; *they are also part of the "today" of salvation*. This making present comes about above all in the Liturgy: what God accomplished centuries ago did not only affect the direct witnesses of those events; it continues to affect people in every age with its gift of grace. To some extent this is also true of every other devout approach to those events: to "remember" them in a spirit of faith and love is to be open to the grace which Christ won for us by the mysteries of his life, death and resurrection.

Consequently, while it must be reaffirmed with the Second Vatican Council that the Liturgy, as the exercise of the priestly office of Christ and an act of public worship, is "the summit to which the activity of the Church is directed and the font from

---

[14]Apostolic Exhortation *Marialis Cultus* (2 February 1974), 47: AAS (1974), 156.

which all its power flows",[15] it is also necessary to recall that the spiritual life "is not limited solely to participation in the liturgy. Christians, while they are called to prayer in common, must also go to their own rooms to pray to their Father in secret (cf. Mt 6:6); indeed, according to the teaching of the Apostle, they must pray without ceasing (cf.1Thes 5:17)".[16] The Rosary, in its own particular way, is part of this varied panorama of "ceaseless" prayer. If the Liturgy, as the activity of Christ and the Church, is *a saving action par excellence*, the Rosary too, as a "meditation" with Mary on Christ, is *a salutary contemplation.* By immersing us in the mysteries of the Redeemer's life, it ensures that what he has done and what the liturgy makes present is profoundly assimilated and shapes our existence.

Learning Christ from Mary

14. Christ is the supreme Teacher, the revealer and the one revealed. It is not just a question of learning what he taught but of *"learning him"*. In this regard could we have any better teacher than Mary? From the divine standpoint, the Spirit is the interior teacher who leads us to the full truth of Christ (cf. Jn 14:26; 15:26; 16:13). But among creatures no one knows Christ better than Mary; no one can introduce us to a profound knowledge of his mystery better than his Mother.

The first of the "signs" worked by Jesus - the changing of water into wine at the marriage in Cana - clearly presents Mary in the guise of a teacher, as she urges the servants to do what Jesus commands (cf. Jn 2:5). We can imagine that she would have done likewise for the disciples after Jesus' Ascension, when she joined them in awaiting the Holy Spirit and supported them in their first mission. Contemplating the scenes of the Rosary in union with Mary is a means of learning from her to "read" Christ, to discover his secrets and to understand his message.

This school of Mary is all the more effective if we con-

---

[15]Constitution on the Sacred Liturgy Sacrosanctum Concilium, 10.
[16]Ibid., 12.

sider that she teaches by obtaining for us in abundance the gifts of the Holy Spirit, even as she offers us the incomparable example of her own "pilgrimage of faith".[17] As we contemplate each mystery of her Son's life, she invites us to do as she did at the Annunciation: to ask humbly the questions which open us to the light, in order to end with the obedience of faith: "Behold I am the handmaid of the Lord; be it done to me according to your word" (Lk 1:38).

Being conformed to Christ with Mary

15. Christian spirituality is distinguished by the disciple's commitment to become conformed ever more fully to his Master (cf. Rom 8:29; Phil 3:10,12). The outpouring of the Holy Spirit in Baptism grafts the believer like a branch onto the vine which is Christ (cf. Jn 15:5) and makes him a member of Christ's mystical Body (cf.1Cor 12:12; Rom 12:5). This initial unity, however, calls for a growing assimilation which will increasingly shape the conduct of the disciple in accordance with the "mind" of Christ: "Have this mind among yourselves, which was in Christ Jesus" (Phil 2:5). In the words of the Apostle, we are called "to put on the Lord Jesus Christ" (cf. Rom 13:14; *Gal* 3:27).

In the spiritual journey of the Rosary, based on the constant contemplation - in Mary's company - of the face of Christ, this demanding ideal of being conformed to him is pursued through an association which could be described in terms of friendship. We are thereby enabled to enter naturally into Christ's life and as it were to share his deepest feelings. In this regard Blessed Bartolo Longo has written: "Just as two friends, frequently in each other's company, tend to develop similar habits, so too, by holding familiar converse with Jesus and the Blessed Virgin, by meditating on the mysteries of the Rosary and by living the same life in Holy Communion, we can become, to the extent of our lowliness, similar to them and can learn from these supreme models a life of humility, poverty, hiddenness, patience

---

[17]Second Vatican Ecumenical Council, Dogmatic Constitution on the Church *Lumen Gentium*, 58.

and perfection."[18]

In this process of being conformed to Christ in the Rosary, we entrust ourselves in a special way to the maternal care of the Blessed Virgin. She who is both the Mother of Christ and a member of the Church, indeed her "pre-eminent and altogether singular member",[19] is at the same time the "Mother of the Church". As such, she continually brings to birth children for the mystical Body of her Son. She does so through her intercession, imploring upon them the inexhaustible outpouring of the Spirit. Mary is *the perfect icon of the motherhood of the Church.*

The Rosary mystically transports us to Mary's side as she is busy watching over the human growth of Christ in the home of Nazareth. This enables her to train us and to mold us with the same care, until Christ is "fully formed" in us (cf. Gal 4:19). This role of Mary, totally grounded in that of Christ and radically subordinated to it, "in no way obscures or diminishes the unique mediation of Christ, but rather shows its power".[20] This is the luminous principle expressed by the Second Vatican Council which I have so powerfully experienced in my own life and have made the basis of my episcopal motto: *Totus Tuus.*[21] The motto is of course inspired by the teaching of Saint Louis Marie Grignion de Montfort, who explained in the following words Mary's role in the process of our configuration to Christ: "*Our entire perfection consists in being conformed, united and consecrated to Jesus Christ.* Hence the most perfect of all devotions is undoubtedly that which conforms, unites and consecrates us most perfectly to Jesus Christ. Now, since Mary is of all creatures the one most conformed to Jesus Christ, it follows that among all devotions, that which most consecrates and conforms a soul to our Lord is devotion to Mary, his Holy Mother, and that the more a soul is consecrated to her the more will it be consecrated to Jesus

---

[18] I Quindici Sabati del Santissimo Rosario, 27th ed., Pompei, 1916, 27.

[19] Second Vatican Ecumenical Council, Dogmatic Constitution on the Church Lumen Gentium, 53.

[20] Ibid., 60.

[21] Cf. First Radio Address Urbi et Orbi (17 October 1978): AAS 70 (1978), 927.

Christ."[22] Never as in the Rosary do the life of Jesus and that of Mary appear so deeply joined. Mary lives only in Christ and for Christ!

Praying to Christ with Mary

16. Jesus invited us to turn to God with insistence and the confidence that we will be heard: "Ask, and it will be given to you; seek, and you will find; knock, and it will be opened to you" (Mt 7:7). The basis for this power of prayer is the goodness of the Father, but also the mediation of Christ himself (cf. 1Jn 2:1) and the working of the Holy Spirit who "intercedes for us" according to the will of God (cf. Rom 8:26-27). For "we do not know how to pray as we ought" (Rom 8:26), and at times we are not heard "because we ask wrongly" (cf. Jas 4:2-3).

In support of the prayer which Christ and the Spirit cause to rise in our hearts, Mary intervenes with her maternal intercession. "The prayer of the Church is sustained by the prayer of Mary".[23] If Jesus, the one Mediator, is the Way of our prayer, then Mary, his purest and most transparent reflection, shows us the Way. "Beginning with Mary's unique cooperation with the working of the Holy Spirit, the Churches developed their prayer to the Holy Mother of God, centering it on the person of Christ manifested in his mysteries".[24] At the wedding of Cana the Gospel clearly shows the power of Mary's intercession as she makes known to Jesus the needs of others: "They have no wine" (Jn 2:3).

The Rosary is both meditation and supplication. Insistent prayer to the Mother of God is based on confidence that her maternal intercession can obtain all things from the heart of her Son. She is "all-powerful by grace", to use the bold expression, which needs to be properly understood, of Blessed Bartolo Longo in his *Supplication to Our Lady*.[25] This is a conviction which,

---

[22]*Treatise on True Devotion to the Blessed Virgin Mary.*
[23]*Catechism of the Catholic Church*, 2679.
[24]*Ibid.*, 2675.
[25]The *Supplication to the Queen of the Holy Rosary* was composed

beginning with the Gospel, has grown ever more firm in the experience of the Christian people. The supreme poet Dante expresses it marvellously in the lines sung by Saint Bernard: "Lady, thou art so great and so powerful, that whoever desires grace yet does not turn to thee, would have his desire fly without wings".[26] When in the Rosary we plead with Mary, the sanctuary of the Holy Spirit (cf. Lk 1:35), she intercedes for us before the Father who filled her with grace and before the Son born of her womb, praying with us and for us.

Proclaiming Christ with Mary

17. The Rosary is also a path of proclamation and increasing knowledge, in which the mystery of Christ is presented again and again at different levels of the Christian experience. Its form is that of a prayerful and contemplative presentation, capable of forming Christians according to the heart of Christ. When the recitation of the Rosary combines all the elements needed for an effective meditation, especially in its communal celebration in parishes and shrines, it can present *a significant catechetical opportunity* which pastors should use to advantage. In this way too Our Lady of the Rosary continues her work of proclaiming Christ. The history of the Rosary shows how this prayer was used in particular by the Dominicans at a difficult time for the Church due to the spread of heresy. Today we are facing new challenges. Why should we not once more have recourse to the Rosary, with the same faith as those who have gone before us? The Rosary retains all its power and continues to be a valuable pastoral resource for every good evangelizer.

---

by Blessed Bartolo Longo in 1883 in response to the appeal of Pope Leo XIII, made in his first Encyclical on the Rosary, for the spiritual commitment of all Catholics in combating social ills. It is solemnly recited twice yearly, in May and October.
[26]Divina Commedia, Paradiso XXXIII, 13-15.

CHAPTER II

MYSTERIES OF CHRIST - MYSTERIES OF HIS MOTHER

The Rosary, "a compendium of the Gospel"

18. The only way to approach the contemplation of Christ's face is by listening in the Spirit to the Father's voice, since "no one knows the Son except the Father" (Mt 11:27). In the region of Caesarea Philippi, Jesus responded to Peter's confession of faith by indicating the source of that clear intuition of his identity: "Flesh and blood has not revealed this to you, but my Father who is in heaven" (Mt 16:17). What is needed, then, is a revelation from above. In order to receive that revelation, attentive listening is indispensable: *"Only the experience of silence and prayer* offers the proper setting for the growth and development of a true, faithful and consistent knowledge of that mystery."[27]

The Rosary is one of the traditional paths of Christian prayer directed to the contemplation of Christ's face. Pope Paul VI described it in these words: "As a Gospel prayer, centred on the mystery of the redemptive Incarnation, the Rosary is a prayer with a clearly Christological orientation. Its most char- acteristic element, in fact, the litany- like succession of *Hail Marys*, becomes in itself an unceasing praise of Christ, who is the ultimate object both of the Angel's announcement and of the greeting of the Mother of John the Baptist: 'Blessed is the fruit of your womb' (Lk 1:42). We would go further and say that the succession of *Hail Mary*s constitutes the warp on which is woven the contemplation of the mysteries. The Jesus that each *Hail Mary* recalls is the same Jesus whom the succession of mysteries proposes to us now as the Son of God, now as the Son of the Virgin."[28]

A proposed addition to the traditional pattern

19. Of the many mysteries of Christ's life, only a few are

indicated by the Rosary in the form that has become generally established with the seal of the Church's approval. The selection was determined by the origin of the prayer, which was based on the number 150, the number of the Psalms in the Psalter.

I believe, however, that to bring out fully the Christological depth of the Rosary it would be suitable to make an addition to the traditional pattern which, while left to the freedom of individuals and communities, could broaden it to include *the mysteries of Christ's public ministry between his Baptism and his Passion.* In the course of those mysteries we contemplate important aspects of the person of Christ as the definitive revelation of God. Declared the beloved Son of the Father at the Baptism in the Jordan, Christ is the one who announces the coming of the Kingdom, bears witness to it in his works and proclaims its demands. It is during the years of his public ministry that *the mystery of Christ is most evidently a mystery of light*: "While I am in the world, I am the light of the world" (Jn 9:5).

Consequently, for the Rosary to become more fully a "compendium of the Gospel", it is fitting to add, following reflection on the Incarnation and the hidden life of Christ (the joyful mysteries) and before focusing on the sufferings of his Passion (the sorrowful mysteries) and the triumph of his Resurrection (the glorious mysteries), a meditation on certain particularly significant moments in his public ministry (the mysteries of light). This addition of these new mysteries, without prejudice to any essential aspect of the prayer's traditional format, is meant to give it fresh life and to enkindle renewed interest in the Rosary's place within Christian spirituality as a true doorway to the depths of the Heart of Christ, ocean of joy and of light, of suffering and of glory.

---

[27] John Paul II, Apostolic Letter *Novo Millennio Ineunte* (6 January 2001), 20: AAS 93 (2001), 279.

[28] Apostolic Exhortation *Marialis Cultus* (2 February 1974), 46: AAS 6 (1974), 155.

The Joyful Mysteries

20. The first five decades, the "joyful mysteries", are marked by *the joy radiating from the event of the Incarnation.* This is clear from the very first mystery, the Annunciation, where Gabriel's greeting to the Virgin of Nazareth is linked to an invitation to messianic joy: "Rejoice, Mary". The whole of salvation history, in some sense the entire history of the world, has led up to this greeting. If it is the Father's plan to unite all things in Christ (cf. Eph 1:10), then the whole of the universe is in some way touched by the divine favour with which the Father looks upon Mary and makes her the Mother of his Son. The whole of humanity, in turn, is embraced by the fiat with which she readily agrees to the will of God.

Exultation is the keynote of the encounter with Elizabeth, where the sound of Mary's voice and the presence of Christ in her womb cause John to "leap for joy" (cf. Lk 1:44). Gladness also fills the scene in Bethlehem, when the birth of the divine Child, the Saviour of the world, is announced by the song of the angels and proclaimed to the shepherds as "news of great joy" (Lk 2:10).

The final two mysteries, while preserving this climate of joy, already point to the drama yet to come. The Presentation in the Temple not only expresses the joy of the Child's consecration and the ecstasy of the aged Simeon; it also records the prophecy that Christ will be a "sign of contradiction" for Israel and that a sword will pierce his mother's heart (cf Lk 2:34-35). Joy mixed with drama marks the fifth mystery, the finding of the twelve-year-old Jesus in the Temple. Here he appears in his divine wisdom as he listens and raises questions, already in effect one who "teaches". The revelation of his mystery as the Son wholly dedicated to his Father's affairs proclaims the radical nature of the Gospel, in which even the closest of human relationships are challenged by the absolute demands of the Kingdom. Mary and

Joseph, fearful and anxious, "did not understand" his words (Lk 2:50).

To meditate upon the "joyful" mysteries, then, is to enter into the ultimate causes and the deepest meaning of Christian joy. It is to focus on the realism of the mystery of the Incarnation and on the obscure foreshadowing of the mystery of the saving Passion. Mary leads us to discover the secret of Christian joy, reminding us that Christianity is, first and foremost, *euangelion*, "good news", which has as its heart and its whole content the person of Jesus Christ, the Word made flesh, the one Saviour of the world.

The Mysteries of Light

21. Moving on from the infancy and the hidden life in Nazareth to the public life of Jesus, our contemplation brings us to those mysteries which may be called in a special way "mysteries of light". Certainly the whole mystery of Christ is a mystery of light. He is the "light of the world" (Jn 8:12). Yet this truth emerges in a special way during the years of his public life, when he proclaims the Gospel of the Kingdom. In proposing to the Christian community five significant moments - "luminous" mysteries - during this phase of Christ's life, I think that the following can be fittingly singled out: (1) his Baptism in the Jordan, (2) his self-manifestation at the wedding of Cana, (3) his proclamation of the Kingdom of God, with his call to conversion, (4) his Transfiguration, and finally, (5) his institution of the Eucharist, as the sacramental expression of the Paschal Mystery.

Each of these mysteries is *a revelation of the Kingdom now present in the very person of Jesus*. The Baptism in the Jordan is first of all a mystery of light. Here, as Christ descends into the waters, the innocent one who became "sin" for our sake (cf. 2 Cor 5:21), the heavens open wide and the voice of the Father declares him the beloved Son (cf. Mt 3:17 and parallels), while the Spirit descends on him to invest him with the mission which he is to carry out. Another mystery of light is the first of the signs, given at Cana (cf. Jn 2:1- 12), when Christ changes water into wine and opens the hearts of the disciples to faith, thanks to the intervention of Mary, the first among believers. Another mystery of light is the preaching by which Jesus proclaims the coming of the Kingdom of God, calls to conversion (cf. Mk 1:15) and forgives the sins of all who draw near to him in humble trust (cf. Mk 2:3-13; Lk 7:47- 48): the inauguration of that ministry of mercy which he continues to exercise until the end of the world, particularly through the Sacrament of Reconciliation which he has entrusted to his Church (cf. Jn 20:22-23). The mystery of light *par excellence* is the Transfiguration, traditionally believed to have taken place on Mount Tabor. The glory of the Godhead shines forth from the face of Christ as the Father commands the astonished Apostles to "listen to him" (cf. Lk 9:35 and parallels) and to prepare to experience with him the agony of the Passion, so as to come with him to the joy of the Resurrection and a life transfigured by the Holy Spirit. A final mystery of light is the institution of the Eucharist, in which Christ offers his body and blood as food under the signs of bread and wine, and testifies "to the end" his love for humanity (Jn 13:1), for whose salvation he will offer himself in sacrifice.

In these mysteries, apart from the miracle at Cana, the *presence of Mary remains in the background.* The Gospels make only the briefest reference to her occasional presence at one moment or other during the preaching of Jesus (cf. Mk 3:31-5; Jn 2:12), and they give no indication that she was present at the Last Supper and the institution of the Eucharist. Yet the role she assumed at Cana in some way accompanies Christ throughout his ministry. The revelation made directly by the Father at the Baptism in the Jordan and echoed by John the Baptist is placed upon Mary's lips at Cana, and it becomes the great maternal counsel which Mary addresses to the Church of every age: "Do whatever he tells you" (Jn 2:5). This counsel is a fitting introduction to the words and signs of Christ's public ministry and it forms the Marian foundation of all the "mysteries of light".

The Sorrowful Mysteries

22. The Gospels give great prominence to the sorrowful mysteries of Christ. From the beginning Christian piety, especially during the Lenten devotion of the *Way of the Cross*, has focused on the individual moments of the Passion, realizing that here is found *the culmination of the revelation of God's love* and the source of our salvation. The Rosary selects certain moments from the Passion, inviting the faithful to contemplate them in their hearts and to relive them. The sequence of meditations begins with Gethsemane, where Christ experiences a moment of great anguish before the will of the Father, against which the weakness of the flesh would be tempted to rebel. There Jesus encounters all the temptations and confronts all the sins of humanity, in order to say to the Father: "Not my will but yours be done" (Lk 22:42 and parallels). This "Yes" of Christ reverses the "No" of our first parents in the Garden of Eden. And the cost of this faithfulness to the Father's will is made clear in the following mysteries; by his scourging, his crowning with thorns, his carrying the Cross and his death on the Cross, the Lord is cast into the most abject suffering: *Ecce homo!*

This abject suffering reveals not only the love of God but also the meaning of man himself.

Ecce homo: the meaning, origin and fulfillment of man is to be found in Christ, the God who humbles himself out of love "even unto death, death on a cross" (Phil 2:8). The sorrowful mysteries help the believer to relive the death of Jesus, to stand at the foot of the Cross beside Mary, to enter with her into the depths of God's love for man and to experience all its life-giving power.

The Glorious Mysteries

23. "The contemplation of Christ's face cannot stop at the image of the Crucified One. He is the Risen One!"[29] The Rosary has always expressed this knowledge born of faith and invited the believer to pass beyond the darkness of the Passion in order

to gaze upon Christ's glory in the Resurrection and Ascension. Contemplating the Risen One, Christians *rediscover the reasons for their own faith* (cf. 1 Cor 15:14) and relive the joy not only of those to whom Christ appeared - the Apostles, Mary Magdalene and the disciples on the road to Emmaus - but also *the joy of Mary*, who must have had an equally intense experience of the new life of her glorified Son. In the Ascension, Christ was raised in glory to the right hand of the Father, while Mary herself would be raised to that same glory in the Assumption, enjoying beforehand, by a unique privilege, the destiny reserved for all the just at the resurrection of the dead. Crowned in glory - as she appears in the last glorious mystery - Mary shines forth as Queen of the Angels and Saints, the anticipation and the supreme realization of the eschatological state of the Church.

At the centre of this unfolding sequence of the glory of the Son and the Mother, the Rosary sets before us the third glorious mystery, Pentecost, which reveals the face of the Church as a family gathered together with Mary, enlivened by the powerful outpouring of the Spirit and ready for the mission of evangeli-zation. The contemplation of this scene, like that of the other glorious mysteries, ought to lead the faithful to an ever greater appreciation of their new life in Christ, lived in the heart of the Church, a life of which the scene of Pentecost itself is the great "icon". The glorious mysteries thus lead the faithful to *greater hope for the eschatological goal* towards which they journey as members of the pilgrim People of God in history. This can only impel them to bear courageous witness to that "good news" which gives meaning to their entire existence.

From "mysteries" to the "Mystery": Mary's way

24. The cycles of meditation proposed by the Holy Rosary are by no means exhaustive, but they do bring to mind what is essential and they awaken in the soul a thirst for a knowledge of Christ continually nourished by the pure source of the Gospel. Every individual event in the life of Christ, as narrated by the evangelists, is resplendent with the Mystery that surpasses all

understanding (cf. Eph 3:19): the Mystery of the Word made flesh, in whom "all the fullness of God dwells bodily" (Col 2:9). For this reason the Catechism of the Catholic Church places great emphasis on the mysteries of Christ, pointing out that "everything in the life of Jesus is a sign of his Mystery."[30] The *"duc in altum"* of the Church of the third millennium will be determined by the ability of Christians to enter into the "perfect knowledge of God's mystery, of Christ, in whom are hidden all the treasures of wisdom and knowledge" (Col 2:2-3). The Letter to the Ephesians makes this heartfelt prayer for all the baptized: "May Christ dwell in your hearts through faith, so that you, being rooted and grounded in love, may have power. . .to know the love of Christ which surpasses knowledge, that you may be filled with all the fullness of God" (3:17-19).

The Rosary is at the service of this idea; it offers the "secret" which leads easily to a profound and inward knowledge of Christ. We might call it *Mary's way*. It is the way of the example of the Virgin of Nazareth, a woman of faith, of silence, of attentive listening. It is also the way of a Marian devotion inspired by knowledge of the inseparable bond between Christ and his Blessed Mother: *the mysteries of Christ* are also in some sense *the mysteries of his Mother,* even when they do not involve her directly, for she lives from him and through him. By making our own the words of the Angel Gabriel and Saint Elizabeth contained in the *Hail Mary*, we find ourselves constantly drawn to seek out afresh in Mary, in her arms and in her heart, the "blessed fruit of her womb" (cf Lk 1:42).

Mystery of Christ, mystery of man

25. In my testimony of 1978 mentioned above, where I described the Rosary as my favourite prayer, I used an idea to which I would like to return. I said then that "the simple prayer of the Rosary marks the rhythm of human life".[31]

---

[29]John Paul II, Apostolic Letter *Novo Millennio Ineunte* (6 January 2001), 28: AAS 93 (2001), 284.

In the light of what has been said so far on the mysteries of Christ, it is not difficult to go deeper into this *anthropological significance* of the Rosary, which is far deeper than may appear at first sight. Anyone who contemplates Christ through the various stages of his life cannot fail to perceive in him *the truth about man*. This is the great affirmation of the Second Vatican Council which I have so often discussed in my own teaching since the Encyclical Letter *Redemptor Hominis*: "It is only in the mystery of the Word made flesh that the mystery of man is seen in its true light".[32] The Rosary helps to open up the way to this light. Following in the path of Christ, in whom man's path is "recapitulated",[33] revealed and redeemed, believers come face to face with the image of the true man. Contemplating Christ's birth, they learn of the sanctity of life; seeing the household of Nazareth, they learn the original truth of the family according to God's plan; listening to the Master in the mysteries of his public ministry, they find the light which leads them to enter the Kingdom of God; and following him on the way to Calvary, they learn the meaning of salvific suffering. Finally, contemplating Christ and his Blessed Mother in glory, they see the goal towards which each of us is called, if we allow ourselves to be healed and transformed by the Holy Spirit. It could be said that each mystery of the Rosary, carefully meditated, sheds light on the mystery of man.

At the same time, it becomes natural to bring to this encounter with the sacred humanity of the Redeemer all the problems, anxieties, labours and endeavours which go to make up our lives. "Cast your burden on the Lord and he will sustain you" (*Ps 55:23*). To pray the Rosary is to hand over our burdens to the merciful hearts of Christ and his Mother. Twenty-five years later, thinking back over the difficulties which have also been part of my exercise of the Petrine ministry, I feel the need to say once more, as a warm invitation to everyone to experience it personally: the Rosary does indeed "mark the rhythm of human life", bringing it into harmony with the "rhythm" of God's own life, in the joyful communion of the Holy Trinity, our life's destiny and deepest longing.

CHAPTER III

"FOR ME, TO LIVE IS CHRIST"

The Rosary, a way of assimilating the mystery

26. Meditation on the mysteries of Christ is proposed in the Rosary by means of a method designed to assist in their assimilation. It is a method *based on repetition*. This applies above all to the *Hail Mary*, repeated ten times in each mystery. If this repetition is considered superficially, there could be a temptation to see the Rosary as a dry and boring exercise. It is quite another thing, however, when the Rosary is thought of as an outpouring of that love which tirelessly returns to the person loved with expressions similar in their content but ever fresh in terms of the feeling pervading them.

In Christ, God has truly assumed a "heart of flesh". Not only does God have a divine heart, rich in mercy and in forgiveness, but also a human heart, capable of all the stirrings of affection. If we needed evidence for this from the Gospel, we could easily find it in the touching dialogue between Christ and Peter after the Resurrection: "Simon, son of John, do you love me?" Three times this question is put to Peter, and three times he gives the reply: "Lord, you know that I love you" (cf. Jn 21:15-17). Over and above the specific meaning of this passage, so important for Peter's mission, none can fail to recognize the beauty of this triple repetition, in which the insistent request and the corresponding reply are expressed in terms familiar from the universal experience of human love. To understand the Rosary, one has to enter into the psychological dynamic proper to love.

One thing is clear: although the repeated *Hail Mary* is addressed directly to Mary, it is to Jesus that the act of love is ultimately directed, with her and through her. The repetition is nourished by the desire to be conformed ever more completely to Christ, the true programme of the Christian life. Saint Paul

---

[30]No. 515.

expressed this project with words of fire: "For me to live is Christ and to die is gain" (Phil 1:21). And again: "It is no longer I that live, but Christ lives in me" (Gal 2:20). The Rosary helps us to be conformed ever more closely to Christ until we attain true holiness.

A valid method...

27. We should not be surprised that our relationship with Christ makes use of a method. God communicates himself to us respecting our human nature and its vital rhythms. Hence, while Christian spirituality is familiar with the most sublime forms of mystical silence in which images, words and gestures are all, so to speak, superseded by an intense and ineffable union with God, it normally engages the whole person in all his complex psychological, physical and relational reality.

This becomes apparent in the *Liturgy*. Sacraments and sacramentals are structured as a series of rites which bring into play all the dimensions of the person. The same applies to non-liturgical prayer. This is confirmed by the fact that, in the East, the most characteristic prayer of Christological meditation, centred on the words "Lord Jesus Christ, Son of God, have mercy on me, a sinner"[34] is traditionally linked to the rhythm of breathing; while this practice favours perseverance in the prayer, it also in some way embodies the desire for Christ to become the breath, the soul and the "all" of one's life.

... which can nevertheless be improved

28. I mentioned in my Apostolic Letter *Novo Millennio Ineunte* that the West is now experiencing a renewed demand for meditation, which at times leads to a keen interest in aspects of

[31] Angelus Message of 29 October 1978 : *Insegnamenti*, I (1978), 76.

[32] Second Vatican Ecumenical Council, Pastoral Constitution on the Church in the Modern World *Gaudium et Spes*, 22.

[33] Cf. Saint Irenaeus of Lyons, *Adversus Haereses*, III, 18, 1: PG 7, 932.

other religions.[35] Some Christians, limited in their knowledge of the Christian contemplative tradition, are attracted by those forms of prayer. While the latter contain many elements which are positive and at times compatible with Christian experience, they are often based on ultimately unacceptable premises. Much in vogue among these approaches are methods aimed at attaining a high level of spiritual concentration by using techniques of a psychophysical, repetitive and symbolic nature. The Rosary is situated within this broad gamut of religious phenomena, but it is distinguished by characteristics of its own which correspond to specifically Christian requirements.

In effect, the Rosary is simply *a method of contemplation.* As a method, it serves as a means to an end and cannot become an end in itself. All the same, as the fruit of centuries of experience, this method should not be undervalued. In its favour one could cite the experience of countless Saints. This is not to say, however, that the method cannot be improved. Such is the intent of the addition of the new series of mysteria lucis to the overall cycle of mysteries and of the few suggestions which I am proposing in this Letter regarding its manner of recitation. These suggestions, while respecting the well-established structure of this prayer, are intended to help the faithful to understand it in the richness of its symbolism and in harmony with the demands of daily life. Otherwise there is a risk that the Rosary would not only fail to produce the intended spiritual effects, but even that the beads, with which it is usually said, could come to be regarded as some kind of amulet or magic object, thereby radically distorting their meaning and function.

Announcing each mystery

29. Announcing each mystery, and perhaps even using a suitable icon to portray it, is as it were *to open up a scenario* on which to focus our attention. The words direct the imagination and the mind towards a particular episode or moment in the life of Christ. In the Church's traditional spirituality, the veneration of icons and the many devotions appealing to the senses, as well as

the method of prayer proposed by Saint Ignatius of Loyola in the Spiritual Exercises, make use of visual and imaginative elements (*the compositio loci*), judged to be of great help in concentrating the mind on the particular mystery. This is a methodology, more-over, which *corresponds to the inner logic of the Incarnation*: in Jesus, God wanted to take on human features. It is through his bodily reality that we are led into contact with the mystery of his divinity.

This need for concreteness finds further expression in the announcement of the various mysteries of the Rosary. Obviously these mysteries neither replace the Gospel nor exhaust its content. The Rosary, therefore, is no substitute for *lectio divina*; on the contrary, it presupposes and promotes it. Yet, even though the mysteries contemplated in the Rosary, even with the addition of the *mysteria lucis*, do no more than outline the fundamental ele-ments of the life of Christ, they easily draw the mind to a more expansive reflection on the rest of the Gospel, especially when the Rosary is prayed in a setting of prolonged recollection.

Listening to the word of God

30. In order to supply a Biblical foundation and greater depth to our meditation, it is helpful to follow the announcement of the mystery with *the proclamation of a related Biblical pas-sage*, long or short, depending on the circumstances. No other words can ever match the efficacy of the inspired word. As we listen, we are certain that this is the word of God, spoken for today and spoken "for me".

If received in this way, the word of God can become part of the Rosary's methodology of repetition without giving rise to the ennui derived from the simple recollection of something already well known. It is not a matter of recalling information but *of allowing God to speak*. In certain solemn communal celebra-tions, this word can be appropriately illustrated by a brief com-mentary.

Silence

31. *Listening and meditation are nourished by silence.* After the announcement of the mystery and the proclamation of the word, it is fitting to pause and focus one's attention for a suitable period of time on the mystery concerned, before moving into vocal prayer. A discovery of the importance of silence is one of the secrets of practicing contemplation and meditation. One drawback of a society dominated by technology and the mass media is the fact that silence becomes increasingly difficult to achieve. Just as moments of silence are recommended in the Liturgy, so too in the recitation of the Rosary it is fitting to pause briefly after listening to the word of God, while the mind focuses on the content of a particular mystery.

The "Our Father"

32. After listening to the word and focusing on the mystery, it is natural for *the mind to be lifted up towards the Father.* In each of his mysteries, Jesus always leads us to the Father, for as he rests in the Father's bosom (cf. Jn 1:18) he is continually turned towards him. He wants us to share in his intimacy with the Father, so that we can say with him: "Abba, Father" (Rom 8:15; Gal 4:6). By virtue of his relationship to the Father he makes us brothers and sisters of himself and of one another, communicating to us the Spirit which is both his and the Father's. Acting as a kind of foundation for the Christological and Marian meditation which unfolds in the repetition of the *Hail Mary,* the *Our Father* makes meditation upon the mystery, even when carried out in solitude, an ecclesial experience.

The ten "Hail Marys"

33. This is the most substantial element in the Rosary and also the one which makes it a Marian prayer *par excellence.* Yet

---

[34]*Catechism of the Catholic Church,* 2616.
[35]Cf. No. 33: AAS 93 (2001), 289.

when the *Hail Mary* is properly understood, we come to see clearly that its Marian character is not opposed to its Christological
character, but that it actually emphasizes and increases it. The first
part of the *Hail Mary*, drawn from the words spoken to Mary by
the Angel Gabriel and by Saint Elizabeth, is a contemplation in
adoration of the mystery accomplished in the Virgin of Nazareth.
These words express, so to speak, the wonder of heaven and earth;
they could be said to give us a glimpse of God's own wonderment
as he contemplates his "masterpiece" - the Incarnation of the Son
in the womb of the Virgin Mary. If we recall how, in the Book
of Genesis, God "saw all that he had made" (Gen 1:31), we can
find here an echo of that "pathos with which God, at the dawn
of creation, looked upon the work of his hands".[36] The repetition
of the *Hail Mary* in the Rosary gives us a share in God's own
wonder and pleasure: in jubilant amazement we acknowledge the
greatest miracle of history. Mary's prophecy here finds its fulfillment: "Henceforth all generations will call me blessed" (Lk 1:48).

The centre of gravity in the *Hail Mary,* the hinge as it were
which joins its two parts, is *the name of Jesus.* Sometimes, in hurried recitation, this centre of gravity can be overlooked, and with
it the connection to the mystery of Christ being contemplated. Yet
it is precisely the emphasis given to the name of Jesus and to
his mystery that is the sign of a meaningful and fruitful recitation
of the Rosary. Pope Paul VI drew attention, in his Apostolic
Exhortation *Marialis Cultus*, to the custom in certain regions
of highlighting the name of Christ by the addition of a clause
referring to the mystery being contemplated.[37] This is a praiseworthy custom, especially during public recitation. It gives forceful expression to our faith in Christ, directed to the different
moments of the Redeemer's life. It is at once *a profession of faith*
and an aid in concentrating our meditation, since it facilitates the
process of assimilation to the mystery of Christ inherent in the
repetition of the *Hail Mary*. When we repeat the name of Jesus -
the only name given to us by which we may hope for salvation
(cf. Acts 4:12) - in close association with the name of his Blessed
Mother, almost as if it were done at her suggestion, we set out
on a path of assimilation meant to help us enter more deeply into

the life of Christ.

From Mary's uniquely privileged relationship with Christ, which makes her the Mother of God, *Theotókos*, derives the forcefulness of the appeal we make to her in the second half of the prayer, as we entrust to her maternal intercession our lives and the hour of our death.

The "Gloria"

34. Trinitarian doxology is the goal of all Christian contemplation. For Christ is the way that leads us to the Father in the Spirit. If we travel this way to the end, we repeatedly encounter the mystery of the three divine Persons, to whom all praise, worship and thanksgiving are due. It is important that the *Gloria, the high-point of contemplation*, be given due prominence in the Rosary. In public recitation it could be sung, as a way of giving proper emphasis to the essentially Trinitarian structure of all Christian prayer.

To the extent that meditation on the mystery is attentive and profound, and to the extent that it is enlivened - from one *Hail Mary* to another - by love for Christ and for Mary, the glorification of the Trinity at the end of each decade, far from being a perfunctory conclusion, takes on its proper contemplative tone, raising the mind as it were to the heights of heaven and enabling us in some way to relive the experience of Tabor, a foretaste of the contemplation yet to come: "It is good for us to be here!" (Lk 9:33).

The concluding short prayer

35. In current practice, the Trinitarian doxology is followed by a brief concluding prayer which varies according to local custom. Without in any way diminishing the value of such invocations, it is worthwhile to note that the contemplation of the mysteries could better express their full spiritual fruitfulness if an effort were made to conclude each mystery with *a prayer for the fruits specific to that particular mystery*. In this way the Rosary

would better express its connection with the Christian life. One fine liturgical prayer suggests as much, inviting us to pray that, by meditation on the mysteries of the Rosary, we may come to "imitate what they contain and obtain what they promise". [38]

Such a final prayer could take on a legitimate variety of forms, as indeed it already does. In this way the Rosary can be better adapted to different spiritual traditions and different Christian communities. It is to be hoped, then, that appropriate formulas will be widely circulated, after due pastoral discernment and possibly after experimental use in centres and shrines particularly devoted to the Rosary, so that the People of God may benefit from an abundance of authentic spiritual riches and find nourishment for their personal contemplation.

The Rosary beads

36. The traditional aid used for the recitation of the Rosary is the set of beads. At the most superficial level, the beads often become a simple counting mechanism to mark the succession of *Hail Marys*. Yet they can also take on a symbolism which can give added depth to contemplation.

Here the first thing to note is the way *the beads converge upon the Crucifix*, which both opens and closes the unfolding sequence of prayer. The life and prayer of believers is centred upon Christ. Everything begins from him, everything leads towards him, everything, through him, in the Holy Spirit, attains to the Father.

As a counting mechanism, marking the progress of the prayer, the beads evoke the unending path of contemplation and of Christian perfection. Blessed Bartolo Longo saw them also as a "chain" which links us to God. A chain, yes, but a sweet chain; for sweet indeed is the bond to God who is also our Father. A "filial" chain which puts us in tune with Mary, the "handmaid of the Lord" (Lk 1:38) and, most of all, with Christ himself, who, though he was in the form of God, made himself a "servant" out of love for us (Phil 2:7).

A fine way to expand the symbolism of the beads is to

let them remind us of our many relationships, of the bond of communion and fraternity which unites us all in Christ.

The opening and closing

37. At present, in different parts of the Church, there are many ways to introduce the Rosary. In some places, it is customary to begin with the opening words of Psalm 70: "O God, come to my aid; O Lord, make haste to help me", as if to nourish in those who are praying a humble awareness of their own insufficiency. In other places, the Rosary begins with the recitation of the Creed, as if to make the profession of faith the basis of the contemplative journey about to be undertaken. These and similar customs, to the extent that they prepare the mind for contemplation, are all equally legitimate. The Rosary is then ended with a prayer for the intentions of the Pope, as if to expand the vision of the one praying to embrace all the needs of the Church. It is precisely in order to encourage this ecclesial dimension of the Rosary that the Church has seen fit to grant indulgences to those who recite it with the required dispositions.

If prayed in this way, the Rosary truly becomes a spiritual itinerary in which Mary acts as Mother, Teacher and Guide, sustaining the faithful by her powerful intercession. Is it any wonder, then, that the soul feels the need, after saying this prayer and experiencing so profoundly the motherhood of Mary, to burst forth in praise of the Blessed Virgin, either in that splendid prayer the *Salve Regina* or in the *Litany of Loreto*? This is the crowning moment of an inner journey which has brought the faithful into living contact with the mystery of Christ and his Blessed Mother.

Distribution over time

---

[36]John Paul II, *Letter to Artists* (4 April 1999), 1: AAS 91 (1999), 1155.

[37]Cf. No. 46: AAS 66 (1974), 155. This custom has also been recently praised by the Congregation for Divine Worship and for the Discipline of the Sacraments in its *Direttorio su pietà popolare e liturgia. Principi e orientamenti* (17 December 2001), 201, Vatican City, 2002, 165.

38. The Rosary can be recited in full every day, and there are those who most laudably do so. In this way it fills with prayer the days of many a contemplative, or keeps company with the sick and the elderly who have abundant time at their disposal. Yet it is clear - and this applies all the more if the new series of *mysteria lucis* is included - that many people will not be able to recite more than a part of the Rosary, according to a certain weekly pattern. This weekly distribution has the effect of giving the different days of the week a certain spiritual "colour", by analogy with the way in which the Liturgy colours the different seasons of the liturgical year.

According to current practice, Monday and Thursday are dedicated to the "joyful mysteries", Tuesday and Friday to the "sorrowful mysteries", and Wednesday, Saturday and Sunday to the "glorious mysteries". Where might the "mysteries of light" be inserted? If we consider that the "glorious mysteries" are said on both Saturday and Sunday, and that Saturday has always had a special Marian flavour, the second weekly meditation on the "joyful mysteries", mysteries in which Mary's presence is especially pronounced, could be moved to Saturday. Thursday would then be free for meditating on the "mysteries of light".

This indication is not intended to limit a rightful freedom in personal and community prayer, where account needs to be taken of spiritual and pastoral needs and of the occurrence of particular liturgical celebrations which might call for suitable adaptations. What is really important is that the Rosary should always be seen and experienced as a path of contemplation. In the Rosary, in a way similar to what takes place in the Liturgy, the Christian week, centred on Sunday, the day of Resurrection, becomes a journey through the mysteries of the life of Christ, and he is revealed in the lives of his disciples as the Lord of time and of history.

CONCLUSION

"Blessed Rosary of Mary, sweet chain linking us to God"

39. What has been said so far makes abundantly clear the richness of this traditional prayer, which has the simplicity of a popular devotion but also the theological depth of a prayer suited to those who feel the need for deeper contemplation.

The Church has always attributed particular efficacy to this prayer, entrusting to the Rosary, to its choral recitation and to its constant practice, the most difficult problems. At times when Christianity itself seemed under threat, its deliverance was attributed to the power of this prayer, and Our Lady of the Rosary was acclaimed as the one whose intercession brought salvation.

Today I willingly entrust to the power of this prayer - as I mentioned at the beginning - the cause of peace in the world and the cause of the family.

Peace

40. The grave challenges confronting the world at the start of this new Millennium lead us to think that only an intervention from on high, capable of guiding the hearts of those living in situations of conflict and those governing the destinies of nations, can give reason to hope for a brighter future.

The Rosary is by its nature a prayer for peace, since it consists in the contemplation of Christ, the Prince of Peace, the one who is "our peace" (Eph 2:14). Anyone who assimilates the mystery of Christ - and this is clearly the goal of the Rosary - learns the secret of peace and makes it his life's project. Moreover, by virtue of its meditative character, with the tranquil succession of *Hail Marys*, the Rosary has a peaceful effect on those who pray it, disposing them to receive and experience in their innermost depths, and to spread around them, that true peace which is the special gift of the Risen Lord (cf. Jn 14:27; 20.21).

The Rosary is also a prayer for peace because of the fruits of charity which it produces. When prayed well in a truly meditative way, the Rosary leads to an encounter with Christ in

---

38"*...concede, quaesumus, ut haec mysteria sacratissimo beatae Mariae Virginis Rosario recolentes, et imitemur quod continent, et quod promittunt assequamur". Missale Romanum 1960, in festo B.M. Virginis a Rosario.*

his mysteries and so cannot fail to draw attention to the face of Christ in others, especially in the most afflicted. How could one possibly contemplate the mystery of the Child of Bethlehem, in the joyful mysteries, without experiencing the desire to welcome, defend and promote life, and to shoulder the burdens of suffering children all over the world? How could one possibly follow in the footsteps of Christ the Revealer, in the mysteries of light, without resolving to bear witness to his "Beatitudes" in daily life? And how could one contemplate Christ carrying the Cross and Christ Crucified, without feeling the need to act as a "Simon of Cyrene" for our brothers and sisters weighed down by grief or crushed by despair? Finally, how could one possibly gaze upon the glory of the Risen Christ or of Mary Queen of Heaven, without yearning to make this world more beautiful, more just, more closely conformed to God's plan?

In a word, by focusing our eyes on Christ, the Rosary also makes us peacemakers in the world. By its nature as an insistent choral petition in harmony with Christ's invitation to "pray ceaselessly" (Lk 18:1), the Rosary allows us to hope that, even today, the difficult "battle" for peace can be won. Far from offering an escape from the problems of the world, the Rosary obliges us to see them with responsible and generous eyes, and obtains for us the strength to face them with the certainty of God's help and the firm intention of bearing witness in every situation to "love, which binds everything together in perfect harmony" (Col 3:14).

The family: parents...

41. As a prayer for peace, the Rosary is also, and always has been, a prayer of and for the family. At one time this prayer was particularly dear to Christian families, and it certainly brought them closer together. It is important not to lose this precious inheritance. We need to return to the practice of family prayer and prayer for families, continuing to use the Rosary.

In my Apostolic Letter *Novo Millennio Ineunte* I encouraged the celebration of the *Liturgy of the Hours* by the lay faithful in the ordinary life of parish communities and Christian groups;[39]

I now wish to do the same for the Rosary. These two paths of Christian contemplation are not mutually exclusive; they complement one another. I would therefore ask those who devote themselves to the pastoral care of families to recommend heartily the recitation of the Rosary.

The family that prays together stays together. The Holy Rosary, by age-old tradition, has shown itself particularly effective as a prayer which brings the family together. Individual family members, in turning their eyes towards Jesus, also regain the ability to look one another in the eye, to communicate, to show solidarity, to forgive one another and to see their covenant of love renewed in the Spirit of God.

Many of the problems facing contemporary families, especially in economically developed societies, result from their increasing difficulty in communicating. Families seldom manage to come together, and the rare occasions when they do are often taken up with watching television. To return to the recitation of the family Rosary means filling daily life with very different images, images of the mystery of salvation: the image of the Redeemer, the image of his most Blessed Mother. The family that recites the Rosary together reproduces something of the atmosphere of the household of Nazareth: its members place Jesus at the centre, they share his joys and sorrows, they place their needs and their plans in his hands, they draw from him the hope and the strength to go on.

... and children

42. It is also beautiful and fruitful to entrust to this prayer *the growth and development of children.* Does the Rosary not follow the life of Christ, from his conception to his death, and then to his Resurrection and his glory? Parents are finding it ever more difficult to follow the lives of their children as they grow to maturity. In a society of advanced technology, of mass communications and globalization, everything has become hurried, and the cultural distance between generations is growing ever greater. The most diverse messages and the most unpredictable experiences rapidly

make their way into the lives of children and adolescents, and parents can become quite anxious about the dangers their children face. At times parents suffer acute disappointment at the failure of their children to resist the seductions of the drug culture, the lure of an unbridled hedonism, the temptation to violence, and the manifold expressions of meaninglessness and despair.

To pray the Rosary *for children*, and even more, *with children*, training them from their earliest years to experience this daily "pause for prayer" with the family, is admittedly not the solution to every problem, but it is a spiritual aid which should not be underestimated. It could be objected that the Rosary seems hardly suited to the taste of children and young people of today. But perhaps the objection is directed to an impoverished method of praying it. Furthermore, without prejudice to the Rosary's basic structure, there is nothing to stop children and young people from praying it - either within the family or in groups - with appropriate symbolic and practical aids to understanding and appreciation. Why not try it? With God's help, a pastoral approach to youth which is positive, impassioned and creative - as shown by the World Youth Days! - is capable of achieving quite remarkable results. If the Rosary is well presented, I am sure that young people will once more surprise adults by the way they make this prayer their own and recite it with the enthusiasm typical of their age group.

The Rosary, a treasure to be rediscovered

43. Dear brothers and sisters! A prayer so easy and yet so rich truly deserves to be rediscovered by the Christian community. Let us do so, especially this year, as a means of confirming the direction outlined in my Apostolic Letter *Novo Millennio Ineunte*, from which the pastoral plans of so many particular Churches have drawn inspiration as they look to the immediate future.

I turn particularly to you, my dear Brother Bishops, priests and deacons, and to you, pastoral agents in your different ministries: through your own personal experience of the beauty of the Rosary, may you come to promote it with conviction.

I also place my trust in you, theologians: by your sage and rigorous reflection, rooted in the word of God and sensitive to the lived experience of the Christian people, may you help them to discover the Biblical foundations, the spiritual riches and the pastoral value of this traditional prayer.

I count on you, consecrated men and women, called in a particular way to contemplate the face of Christ at the school of Mary.

I look to all of you, brothers and sisters of every state of life, to you, Christian families, to you, the sick and elderly, and to you, young people: *confidently take up the Rosary once again.* Rediscover the Rosary in the light of Scripture, in harmony with the Liturgy, and in the context of your daily lives.

May this appeal of mine not go unheard! At the start of the twenty-fifth year of my Pontificate, I entrust this Apostolic Letter to the loving hands of the Virgin Mary, *prostrating myself in spirit before her image in the splendid Shrine built for her by Blessed Bartolo Longo*, the apostle of the Rosary. I willingly make my own the touching words with which he concluded his well-known *Supplication to the Queen of the Holy Rosary*: "O Blessed Rosary of Mary, sweet chain which unites us to God, bond of love which unites us to the angels, tower of salvation against the assaults of Hell, safe port in our universal shipwreck, we will never abandon you. You will be our comfort in the hour of death: yours our final kiss as life ebbs away. And the last word from our lips will be your sweet name, O Queen of the Rosary of Pompei, O dearest Mother, O Refuge of Sinners, O Sovereign Consoler of the Afflicted. May you be everywhere blessed, today and always, on earth and in heaven."

Presented at the Vatican on October 16, 2002 by John Paul II.

Notes

[1] Earle Zeigler, Ph.D., *History of Sport and Physical Education to 1900*, Stipes Publishing Co., Champaign, IL, 1973, 191.

[2] Donna Miller, Kathryn Russell, *Sport: A Contemporary View*, Lea & Febiger, Philadelphia, PA, 1971, p. 91.

[3] David McComb, *Sports: An Illustrated History*, Oxford University Press, Oxford, England, 1998, p. 35.

[4] Robert Feeney, *A Catholic Perspective: Physical Exercise and Sports*, 1st edition, Foreword, Aquinas Press, Arlington, VA 1995, p. 11.

[5] *Thirty Days Magazine*, No. 6, 1996, New York, NY, p. 12.

[6] *L'Osservatore Romano*. Vatican City: August, 2004, p. 1.

[7] Jean-Pierre Torrell, O.P., *St. Thomas Aquinas: The Person and the Work*, Catholic University Press, Washington, D.C., 1996, p. 279.

[8] Thomas O'Meara, O.P. *Thomas: Theologian*, University of Notre Dame Press, Notre Dame, IN, 1997, p. 19.

[9] *Letter of Paul VI for Seventh Century of St. Thomas Aquinas*, Order of Friars Preachers, Rome, Italy, 1975.

[10] *Arlington Catholic Herald*, Arlington, VA, August 12, 2004, p. 24.

[11] Kenneth Cooper, M.D., *The Aerobic Way*, M. Evans & Co., New York, NY, 1977, p. 183.

12 A.G. Sertillanges, O.P., *The Intellectual Life*, Christian Classics, Westminster, MD, 1980, p. 34-35.

13 *The Human Body, Monks of Solesmes*, St. Paul Editions, 1960, p. 74.

14 Ibid., p. 75.

15 *L'Osservatore Romano*, Vatican City, November 1, 2000, p. 2.

16 Donna Miller, Ph.D., *The Philosophic Process in Physical Education*, Lea & Febiger, Philadelphia, PA, 1977, p. 145.

17 Christopher West, *Theology of the Body for Beginners*, Ascension Press, Westchester, PA, 2001, p. 4.

18 Donna Miller, Ph.D., *The Philosophic Process in Physical Education*, Lea & Febiger, Philadelphia, PA, 1977, p. 196.

19 *L'Osservatore Romano*, Vatican City, November 1, 2000, p. 1.

20 *L'Osservatore Romano*, Vatican City, April 24, 1984, p. 4.

21 *In the Mountains with John Paul II*, Urbi Et Orbi Communications, New Hope, KY, 2002, p. 20.

22 Maria Di Lorenzo, *Blessed Pier Giorgio Frassati: An Ordinary Christian*, Pauline Books, Boston, MA, 2004, p. xvi.

23 Luciana Frassati, *A Man of the Beatitudes*, Ignatius Press, San Francisco, CA, 2001, p. 97.

24 Ibid., p. 179.

25 Maria Di Lorenza, *Blessed Pier Giorgio Frassati: An Ordinary Christian*, p. 85.

26 *In the Mountains with John Paul II*, p. 20.

27 *Blessed Pier Giorgio Frassati: An Ordinary Christian*, p. 85.

28 *In the Mountains with John Paul II*, p. 20.

29 *A Man of the Beatitudes*, p. 179.

30 *In the Mountains with John Paul II*, p. 16.

31 *Blessed Pier Giorgio Frassati: An Ordinary Christian*, p. 112.

32 *In the Mountains with John Paul II*, p. 16.

33 *Blessed Pier Giorgio Frassati: An Ordinary Christian*, p. 91.

34 Robert Feeney, *The Rosary: The Little Summa*, Aquinas Press, Arlington, VA, 2003, p. 42.

35 Ibid., p. 44.

36 *Blessed Pier Giorgio Frassati: An Ordinary Christian*, p. 55-56.

37 Ibid., p. 91.

38 *A Man of the Beatitudes*, p. 163.

39 *L'Osservatore Romano*, May 28, 1990, p. 9.

[40] *In the Mountains with John Paul II*, p. 20.

[41] *L'Osservatore Romano*, May 28, 1990, p. 9.

[42] Gabriel Hardy, O.P., *Rediscovering the Rosary*, Veritas Publications, Dublin, Ireland, 1983, p. 9.

[43] John De Marchi, I.M.C., *Fatima: The Full Message*, AMI Press, Washington, NJ, 1986, p. 134.

[44] *The Seers of Fatima*, Secretariado dos Pastorinhos, Fatima, Portugal, January/March, 1996, p. 2

[45] Sister Lucia, "Calls from the Message of Fatima," Secretariado dos Pastorinhos, Fatima, Portugal, 2000, p. 150.

[46] *In the Mountains with John Paul II,* p. 15.

[47] Ibid., p. 16.

[48] Ibid., p. 16.

[49] *L'Osservatore Romano*, June 30, 2004, p. 7.

[50] *L'Osservatore Romano*, July 14, 2004, p. 3.

[51] Kenneth Cooper, M.D., *The Aerobic Way,* M. Evans & Co., Inc., New York, N.Y, 1977, p. 183.

[52] Ronald M. Lawrence, M.D., Ph.D., *Going the Distance*, Jeremy P. Tarcher, Inc., Los Angeles, CA, 1987, p. 18.

[53] Ibid., p. 18.

[54] *L'Osservatore Romano*, January 10, 1983, p. 4.

[55] *The Apostolic Fathers*, CIMA Publishing, N.Y., 1947, p. 125.

[56] Reginald Garrogou-Lagrange, O.P., *The Three Ages of the Interior Life*, Benziger, New York, N.Y., 1938, p. 1.

[57] Karol Wojtyla, *The Way to Christ*, Harper & Row, San Francisco, CA, 1984, p. 74.

[58] St. Francis de Sales, *The Introduction to the Devout Life*, Image Books, Garden City, N.Y., 1972, p. 81.

[59] John Paul II, *The Role of the Christian Family in the Modern World*, Pauline Books, Boston, MA, 1981, p. 88-89.

[60] John Paul II, *The Redeemer of Man*, U.S. Catholic Conference, Washington, D.C., 1979, p. 71.

[61] John Paul II, *The Splendor of Truth*, Pauline Books, Boston, MA, 1993, p. 130.

[62] John Paul II, *A Year with Mary*, Catholic Books Publishing Co., New York, N.Y., 1986, p. 220.

[63] *Inside the Vatican*, New Hope, KY, November 2000, p. 1-2.

[64] Ibid., p. 15.

[65] *Inside the Vatican*, New Hope, KY, April-May 2003, p. 1.

[66] Ibid., p. 8.

Bibliography

Bailey, Covert. *The New Fit or Fat*. Boston, MA: Houghton Mifflin Co., 1991.

Cooper, Kenneth, M.D., M.Ph. *Aerobics*. N.Y., New York: M. Evans & Co., 1968.

Cooper, Kenneth, M.D., M.Ph. *Kid Fitness*. N.Y., New York: Bantam Books, 1991.

Cooper, Kenneth, M.D., M.Ph. *The Aerobics Program for Total Well-Being*. N.Y., New York: Bantam Books, 1982.

Cooper, Kenneth, M.D., M.Ph. *The Aerobics Way*. N.Y., New York: Bantam Books, 1978.

De Vries, Herbert A. *Fitness After 50*. N.Y., N.Y.: Charles Scribner's & Sons, 1982.

Di Lorenza, Maria. *Blessed Pier Giorgio Frassati - An Ordinary Christian*. Boston, MA: Pauline Books, 2004.

Feeney, Robert. *The Rosary: The Little Summa*. Arlington, VA: Aquinas Press, 2003.

Frassati, Lucianna. *A Man of the Beatitudes*. San Francisco, CA: Ignatius Press, 2001.

Getchell, Bud, Ph.D. *Physical Fitness: A Way of Life*. N.Y., N.Y.: John Wiley & Sons, Inc. 1979.

Getchell, Bud, Ph.D. *Being Fit - A Personal Guide*. N.Y., N.Y.: John Wiley & Sons, 1982.

Glover, Bob and Shepherd, Jack. *The Family Fitness Handbook.* Penguin Books, 1989.

In the Mountains with John Paul II. New Hope, KY: Urbi Et Orbi Communications, 2002.

Lawrence, Ronald, M.D., Ph.D. *Going the Distance.* Los Angeles, CA: Jeremy P. Tarcher, Inc., 1987.

L'Osservatore Roman. Vatican City: 1979-87.

Miller, David and Allen, T. Earl. *Fitness - A Lifetime Commitment.* N.Y., N.Y.: MacMillan Pub. Co., 1990.

Monks of Solesmes. The Human Body. Boston: The Daughters of St. Paul, 1960.

O'Meara, Thomas, O.P. *Thomas Aquinas, Theologian.* Notre Dame, IN: University of Notre Dame, 1997.

Pollock, Michael, Wilmore, Jack, Fox, Samuel. *Health and Fitness Through Physical Activity.* N.Y., N.Y.: John Wiley & Sons, 1978.

Rippe, James, M.D. *The Sports Performance Factors.* N.Y., N.Y.: Putnam Publishing Co., 1986.

Sister Lucia. "Calls from the Message of Fatima." Fatima, Portugal: Secretariada dos Pastorindos, 2000.

Steinhaus, Author, Ph.D. *Toward an Understanding of Health and Physical Education.* Dubuque, IA: Wm. C. Brown, Co., 1963.

Torrell, Jean-Pierre, O.P. *St. Thomas Aquinas: The Person and the Work.* Washington, D.C.: Catholic University Press, 1996.

Van Aaken, Ernst, M.D. *The Van Aaken Method*. Mountain View, CA: World Publication, 1976.

Vitale, Frank. *Individualized Fitness Programs*. Englewood Cliffs, N.J.: Prentice Hall, Inc., 1973.

Wilmore, Jack, Ph.D. *Sensible Fitness*. Champaign, IL: Leisure Press, 1986.